YO-AGX-686

Smart Car Buying & Leasing 101

by Charles DeVorak

VEHICLE INFORMATION SYSTEMS

This publication is designed to provide accurate and authoritative information in regard to the subject matter covered. It is sold with the understanding that the publisher is not engaged in rendering legal, accounting, or other professional service. If legal advice or other expert assistance is required, the service of a competent professional person should be sought.

Publisher: Vehicle Information Systems, Inc.
              6911 South 1300 East, Suite 228
              Salt Lake City, Utah 84047

First printing January 1997

PRINTED IN THE UNITED STATES OF AMERICA

Typesetting, editing and cover design by 19th & Pizzino Advertising: 801/568-1545.

With love I dedicate this book to my mother who has always been an inspiration throughout my life. Your encouragement and coaching has always been appreciated.

The author would like to thank NBC's *The Today Show* for acknowledging the need for this information by having him as their guest Saturday, May 18, 1996, where the contents of his video, *How To Buy A Car Or Truck And Not Get Ripped Off,* were discussed—which inspired this book. The hospitality rendered by the producers and staff at NBC was second to none.

In addition, the exposure on CNBC's *America's Talking* in March 1996 as a guest was duly appreciated. CNBC's staff was very gracious and accommodating. The author wishes to thank the producers as well as the entire staff—especially the host, Brian Tracey.

The author would also like to acknowledge and thank the N.A.D.A. Official Used Car Guide Company and Kelly Blue Book Co. for allowing reprints of their information, namely the N.A.D.A. Official Used Car Guide® and the Kelly Blue Book Residual Value Guide, respectively.

Abbreviations Used in this Book

M.S.R.P. — Manufacturer's Suggested Retail Price

N.A.D.A. — The National Automobile Dealers' Association

Preface

When I became involved in the car industry about seven years ago, I couldn't believe what really took place. I found most consumers get taken advantage of because they lack some "fundamental" and "advanced" knowledge about purchasing a vehicle.

I thought there had to be a better way to educate consumers and create a synergy between car buyers and dealers. My book, *Car Buying & Leasing 101* and video, *How To Buy A Car Or Truck And Not Get Ripped Off,* were created to provide the basic and advanced knowledge consumers need to make educated choices.

Many books and tapes have been produced on the subject, but none have been this comprehensive. This book was created by someone in the business—someone who *really* knows what goes on behind the scenes. I understand the challenges consumers face, as well as the need for the dealership to make a profit on the vehicles they sell.

Unfortunately, the public has become somewhat

confused when purchasing or leasing a vehicle. As a result, the entire process of buying a car or truck has become a dreadful experience for many consumers. This book will make it a pleasant experience and take the mystery out of buying or leasing a car.

In this book, *I set the record straight and educate you, the buyer.*

Everyone who buys (or leases) a vehicle should read *Car Buying & Leasing 101* because it makes car buying (or leasing) easier. I've had a large cross section of consumers from all walks of life purchase my video, *How To Buy A Car Or Truck And Not Get Ripped Off*—which can be found on the shelves of numerous libraries nationwide. You'll even find it in schools. I highly suggest it for all those of car buying age. (To order, please see ad in back of book.)

Car Buying & Leasing 101 is a companion to the video. One third of the book's contents deal with leasing, and the entire book is designed to be used as a ready reference. You may want to take the book with you when you shop for a vehicle.

In this book you'll find answers to many of your questions. You'll have the entire buying process clearly explained to you. This is not a "kick-the-tires, check-the-oil, how-to-road-test-a-vehicle" book. Rather, it talks about the nitty gritty of leasing, buying new or used, "buy-backs," pricing and selling your trade-in, how to properly use the N.A.D.A. Official Used Car Guide®, what to really expect for trade-in values, and more.

I'll also show you how to use the "Kelly Blue Book Residual Guide" for leasing. Leasing is becoming increasingly popular.

The information in this book is formatted into easy-to-understand sections that will walk you through the entire process in purchasing or leasing a vehicle. You're guaranteed to benefit from reading this book.

Some of the topics covered include:
* Leasing
* Buying new or used cars
* Buy-backs
* Pricing or selling a trade-in
* Negotiating the purchase price
* Dealer invoices
* Financing at the dealership or at a bank
* Warranties and other after-market items
* The mark up and profit on after-market items as well as vehicles

As I tell people about *Car Buying & Leasing 101*, the most common responses are: "Where were you when I needed it?" or "I wish I had that a year ago!" or "How can I get a copy?"

Speaking from within the industry, I would much rather sell a vehicle to an educated consumer. The knowledge a consumer can gain from this book would actually make the car salesperson's job much easier. In fact, car salespeople can greatly benefit from this information.

Read this book carefully. In it you'll find all the information you need to properly negotiate a transaction and to help you reach your ultimate goal—securing the best possible deal with the least amount of aggravation!

When I help a customer proceed through the transaction of obtaining a vehicle, I work with them using the process explained in this book. It works well. It has made car buying easy and painless for all my customers—and it'll do the same for you.

Happy car buying (or leasing)!

Charles DeVorak

Contents

Chapter 1: Introduction
–So Ya Wanna Buy a Car?

Most people view buying a new or used vehicle as the least popular experience to endure in life. I've had people say *they would rather visit the dentist or go on a blind date than try to buy a new or used vehicle*—which entails going through the song-and-dance of the salesperson, the back-and-forth of the negotiating, and everything else.

I've heard stories of people going into dealerships and taking *four to seven hours* to buy something. This resulted in the following: they did <u>not</u> get the vehicle they originally wanted, and even worse *they had no idea what they ended up paying for it!*

You can spare yourself *all* of these hassles by arriving at a dealership with *the* knowledge of *exactly* what you want to accomplish. By implementing the strategies and utilizing the advice in this book, *you can be in and out of the dealership in only an hour or two.* The dealer will be happy, you'll be happy, and it will take away the pain and agony of buying a new or used vehicle.

Save hundreds, *even thousands* of dollars on the purchase of your new or used vehicle. Find out what some people already know, and determine what YOU would like to know (and how to use that information)! *Don't be intimidated.* Instead, know what you're doing when you buy or lease your next vehicle.

If you use the consumer guides, buyer's guides, and/or the internet—which are all very good tools— keep in mind that this is only the beginning of the process. These tools may suggest how much the dealer actually pays for the car, but where do you go from there? How do you find out how to get a dealer to really sell a vehicle to you for what you want to pay?

That's the whole concept. It's no secret as to how much it is. The idea is how can *you* get the price *you* want, and know *you* received that price in the final paperwork? After all, most leases do not disclose the purchase price nor the actual value they are giving you for your trade-in. That's the difference between other tools and this book.

Car Buying & Leasing 101 is the *only* information I'm aware of that can help you achieve this.

Chapter 2: The Pros & Cons of Leasing

2

Leasing is becoming more and more popular. You may find it a better choice than purchasing a vehicle. After reading this chapter, you'll be able to determine for yourself if the pros outweigh the cons when it comes to leasing.

How Does a Lease Really Work?

When you lease a vehicle, you're responsible for the payments of the lease for the term of the lease as it's agreed upon—whether it's 24 months, 36 months, etc. Just because you lease a vehicle doesn't mean you can walk away from it at any time. You do have the right to sell the vehicle on your own during the lease, as long as you pay off the current lease balance.

Similar to conventional financing, in the beginning portion of the lease you will owe more money on the lease payoff than the vehicle will be worth, so be aware of this. Just like buying a car, if you want to get rid of a lease after only four to six months, it will be a challenge financially, and you'll incur some additional early payoff penalties. The basic idea of a lease is paying for the portion of the vehicle that you "use up," meaning the amount it depreciates and the wear and tear you put on it while it's in your possession.

It's important that you understand leases because they are somewhat complicated, and unknowingly you can spend more money on a lease than you think you are spending.

Advantages of Leasing

- ◆ You only pay for the portion of the vehicle you actually use.
- ◆ With a lease you will be driving a new vehicle complete with a factory warranty (that translates to minimum repair bills).
- ◆ Leasing is the most economical choice if you want a different vehicle every two or three years.
- ◆ Leasing keeps you out of the used car business.
- ◆ With a lease you only pay sales tax on the monthly payment. You do not pay sales tax on the total price of the vehicle.

- ◆ You provide normal service for the vehicle (such as oil changes, etc.).
- ◆ Leasing is just like ownership, however, you only really own a car when it's paid off.

Residual Value

Let's start explaining leasing with *residual value,* which is a buzz word in leasing. It may also be referred to as *lease end value, future value* or *guaranteed future value.*

The residual value is simply *the amount of the car you do not pay for.* It's the left over value that exists in the car after you use it. *It's the portion of the car that you do not use up.* In Appendix A you'll find examples of residual value guide charts for March and April of 1996. The lease residual guide changes every two months, so use the pages in Appendix A to familiarize yourself with it, but *make certain you use a current guide at the time you sign your lease.* You can actually ask to see the one at your bank. Banks generally have access to these guides.

For example, if you lease a 1996 Ford Taurus with a M.S.R.P. of $20,000, the residual value will be a percentage of the $20,000. By using the lease residual guide (which is what the dealers and leasing companies use), they establish the residual value for the Ford Taurus—which currently is 59% after 24 months. So 59% of $20,000 is $11,800. The residual value in March 1996 would be $11,800. In January 1996, the same residual would have probably been 60-62% because the model was newer. Remember, we are forecasting the future value of the vehicle. Therefore, the earlier in the year you lease a vehicle, the greater the value will be when you return it. Conversely, the later in the calendar year you lease, the lower this residual value will be. This 59% which was established in March will be approximately 55% by August. This will have a direct affect on your payment.

If you subtract the residual value from the cost of the vehicle, you will see what portion of the vehicle's value you're paying for. For example:

$20,000.00	M.S.R.P. (Manufacturer's Suggested Retail Price)
-<u>11,800.00</u>	Residual value
$8,200.00	Usage fee (portion you're paying for)

This $8,200 *usage fee* is also known as a *depreciation cost* or *lease charge*. You're paying the vehicle down from $20,000 to $11,800. In addition to this, you'll pay interest on the vehicle as well. You'll also pay interest on the entire vehicle, not just the portion which you use up. A quick acid test to calculate the *approximate* interest you'll be paying will be to first calculate your usage fee. In the case of $8,200, here's what happens:

$8,200 ÷ 2 = $4,100 x 2.75 = $11,275.00

The $11,275 = the usage fee and interest total.

Or, your interest is $1/3$ more than your usage fee.

Next, you need to understand that the residual value is taken against M.S.R.P. and not against your negotiated purchase price. For example, a Ford Explorer or a Chevy blazer may have an M.S.R.P. followed by a package discount of $800 or $1,000 on the window sticker. These are offered by the manufacturers and vary from vehicle type to vehicle type and may also vary throughout the year.

Here's a window sticker example:

$29,000.00	M.S.R.P.
-1,000.00	Package discount
$28,000.00	Purchase price
-1,200.00	Dealer discount (negotiated)
$26,800.00	

Furthermore, the dealer and you may have negotiated this price another $1,200, which will then give you a purchase price of $26,800—significantly less than the M.S.R.P. of $29,000. Now as before, your residual will be structured against the $29,000, but your <u>usage/starting</u> <u>price</u>, or purchase price, will be $26,800. Here's what the numbers look like:

$29,000.00	M.S.R.P.
$26,800.00	Purchase price
$17,980.00	Residual value (62%) of $29,000
$8,820.00	Depreciation cost/usage fee

Now subtract the residual value from the negotiated purchase price:

$26,800.00	Purchase price (usage/starting price)
-<u>17,980.00</u>	Residual value (62%) of $29,000
$8,820.00	Depreciation cost/Usage fee

To calculate the monthly payment, use the leasing formula on the next page. Remember, you'll need a calculator with a built-in leasing formula to figure this. I use an older model HP 12C. There are several models available with step-by-step instructions to walk you through the lease formulas. These are made by numerous manufacturers.

Enter:	10% interest
Enter:	24 months for number of payments
Enter:	$17,980 as future value
Enter:	$26,800 for the agreed upon price as present value (referred to as the cap cost). This also includes an **acquisition fee** of $400. Consequently, adjust your cap cost to $27,200 and enter $27,200 instead of $26,800.
Press:	Payment button (payment = $571)

After you hit the payment button on your leasing calculator, your monthly payment of $571 will appear.

When you use a calculator and figure this lease using 10% interest, the payment will be $571 plus tax:

$13,704.00	($571 x 24 = Total of payments paid out in 24 months)
$8,820.00	Depreciation cost (represents your depreciated or usage amount)
$4,884.00	(The interest plus other lease charges) These will include a lease **acquisition fee**, usually $400-700. This is similar to closing costs and will go to the leasing company. This amount needs to be added to the cap cost in the leasing formula.

The only other item we need to add at this point is the monthly sales tax on the payment. Using a 6.25% tax rate (note: tax rates vary state to state), your tax on each payment would be $35.69.

$571.00	Monthly payment
+35.69	Sales tax on monthly payment
$606.69	Total monthly payment with sales tax

One advantage of leasing is that you only pay sales tax on the monthly payment, not on the total price of the vehicle.

Now for comparative purposes, I will work a four- and five-year conventional purchase:

Conventional Purchase/Finance (non-lease)

$26,800.00	Purchase price
+1,675.00	Sales tax
$28,475.00	Sub total
-2,500.00	Down payment
$25,975.00	Total to finance

Payment on 48 months at 10%: $653.00

Payment on 60 months at 10%: $547.00

Utilizing the 24-month lease with payments of $606.69, your down payment will only be the first payment plus security deposit and licensing—or approximately $1,250—compared to the $2,500 down payment required for a conventional purchase. If you're financing for 48 months, at the end of 24 months you'll have paid off half, or 50% of your payments. That amount would actually be 50% of the amount financed plus your $2,500 down payment (which has been used up), plus interest.

Four Year Purchase
$653 x 24 months = $15,672
This amount ($15,672) will also be your payoff because you'll have 50% of your payments remaining.

Five Year Purchase
$547 x 24 months = $13,128
On the five-year loan, you'll have paid in $13,128 after 24 months, leaving $19,692 to still pay off, less some of the interest from the last three years of the loan.

At this point, if you want to trade vehicles, you'll be in trouble. This creates a deficit, and I'll show you how. The January 1996 residual value of this $29,000 vehicle is 62%, or $17,980. Chances are the residual value will match your trade-in value at this time. But the payoff on your five-year loan will be $19,692. See the trend? Therefore:

$19,692.00	Payoff (Balance owed)
-17,980.00	Residual value of vehicle/trade-in value
$1,712.00	Deficit created

It's easy to see how this deficit of $1,712 was created. Financing for 48 months instead of 60 months would have been a better situation because your payoff would be only $15,672, less some interest, instead of $19,692. Remember, with the conventional purchase you also put $2,500 cash down, so be sure to factor that amount in your calculation.

When you factor in the additional $2,500 by adding to the total payments made on the vehicle after 24 months, you'll find your true cost of ownership for the two years of payments *on a conventional purchase.*

$2,500.00	Cash down payment
+13,128.00	Amount paid in 24 payments of 60
$15,628.00	(= payments + down payment = true cost of ownership for 24 months)

$2,500.00	Cash down payment
+15,672.00	Amount paid in 24 payments of 48
$18,172.00	(= payments + down payment = true cost of ownership for 24 months)
$1,250.00	1st payment, security deposit, licensing
+13,943.52	($606.24 x 23 lease payments = cost of ownership for a 24-month lease)
$15,193.52	True cost of ownership for the 24-month lease

Do you see now what happened? Go over this again if you need to. This is an example of why it's very easy to get confused at a dealership—especially when things happen at a rapid pace.

If you would have leased the vehicle, you would not have any concerns about a deficit because after 24 months you're done with the vehicle, and your use of it has been paid for.

Now let's compare a two-year lease with a three-year lease. (Incidentally, if you want a different vehicle every two or three years, leasing is your best option. *In addition,* a three-year lease will typically be a better buy than a two-year lease.)

24-month lease		36-month lease
$29,000.00	M.S.R.P.	$29,000.00
26,800.00	Purchase price	26,800.00
17,980.00	Residual value	16,530.00
(62%)		(57%)
$552.00	Payment w/10% interest	$465.00
+34.50	Sales tax	+29.10
$587.00	Monthly payment	$494.00

The payment in this case for the 36-month lease is $93 less per month than the 24-month lease. This will generally be the case because the residual difference between 24 and 36 months is only 5%. In other words, **the vehicle depreciates less between the second and third year** than it does between the day its new and its first and second years. Vehicles take their largest depreciation hit in the first two years and then it slows to between 5-7% per year. After 48 months, the depreciation again accelerates.

On the following page is a depreciation schedule to better illustrate this:

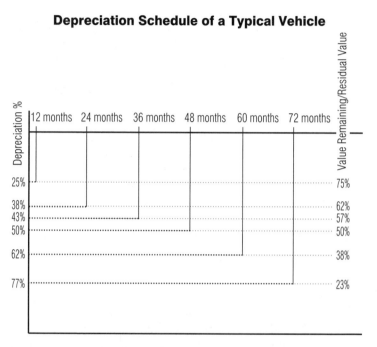

Depreciation Schedule of a Typical Vehicle

Look at the difference between the 24-month residual (62%) compared to the 36-month residual (57%). It's typically a 5% decline in value. This depreciation will be almost the same or another 5-7% drop between 36 months and 48 months, but when the vehicle gets beyond 48 months, the depreciation speeds up again to 10-12% per year. These percentages are taken against M.S.R.P., not necessarily the price you end up paying. The actual percentage of depreciation is greater when calculating it against your actual negotiated purchase price (which is less than the M.S.R.P.).

At this point we have established two important points:

1. A vehicle depreciates faster in the first two years, and

2. The best lease term with the lowest payment is 36 months (three years).

Even though a 24-month lease can be a little more expensive per month, it provides you with the shortest ownership cycle, and usually your factory warranty will out live the length of time you have the vehicle. The manufacturer also prefers you to be in a two-year lease cycle. Why? Because they can build more cars that way. It stands to reason that the more people they get into a two-year trading cycle—instead of three-, four-, or five-year trading cycle—the more vehicles they can produce.

Manufacturers provide additional incentives on 24-month leases not provided on longer leases. In many cases, you will see a manufacturer provide a lease rate, i.e., 2.9%. Even though it's not a true interest rate, it's still a very good deal. The true interest rate attached to true lease rates is usually $1^1/_2$ to 2% higher. In other words, a 2.9% lease rate in real terms is approximately a 4.9% interest rate. It's still a very good deal.

If you're still not totally sold on leasing, and special rates like these are offered on the vehicle you're buying, then take the two-year lease at their 2.9% lease rate and the buy out option after 24 months. You'll save money by using their reduced rate for the first two years of ownership. The purchase option amount is established today, not 24 months from now, consequently, you know ahead of time what your buy out amount will be.

A lease with a pre-established buy out option is the only lease recommended. Stay away from all other leases. I'll say it again: *Stay away from all other leases!* Leases with fair market value buy outs will fluctuate and change. Therefore, you do not want to be involved with these. There's no way you can win because this type of lease grants the leasing company the right to change the purchase option amount and/or to alter your position at the end of the lease. Fair market buy outs mean that if the market value of your automobile changes, the leasing company can charge you more money to buy the vehicle at the end of the lease, or charge additional fees when you finish the lease and return the vehicle.

3 Items Your Lease Must Contain

For your lease to be the correct type, it has to contain three specific items:

1. A guaranteed future value or buy out amount (these are one and the same).

2. The right to sell the vehicle at the end of the lease.

This means selling it to someone else. This option is important because if your car increases in value, you will want to take advantage of this.

For example: if your buy out is $14,000, and you can sell it for $16,000, you just made $2,000. Typically, there are sales tax consequences involved with this process, so be aware of the tax rules of your state. If you found a buyer for the vehicle you're returning, and you purchase another car from the dealership where you originally leased, you should be able to have the dealer assist you—avoiding sales tax on the $14,000 (because you won't be buying it for resale, your customer will be buying it directly from the dealership). However, the buyer for your vehicle will pay sales tax on the $16,000 he is purchasing it for.

3. Your lease must include the right to walk away from the vehicle at the end of the lease term.

In other words, all bets are equal if you are not turning the car in with damage, needed repairs, or excess miles.

A lease is just like ownership: you are responsible for the maintenance, repairs, upkeep and insurance. Normal wear and tear is accepted on lease returns, but damage, etc., is not. You will be assessed for damage when you return the vehicle.

Miles on Leased Vehicles

The miles you drive a leased vehicle are limited, usually from 12,000 to 15,000 miles per year. If you know you're going to drive more than that, arrange to have miles added to your lease and increase the monthly lease payment. This is a better option because you can build in extra miles in your lease for 10-11¢ per mile. Waiting to pay for the extra miles when you return the vehicle will cost you more. If you pay for them when you return the vehicle, you'll be assessed 15¢ a mile (instead of 10-11¢). If you know you're going to purchase the vehicle, you cannot be assessed for the miles—so it doesn't matter. However, don't fool yourself. You're still better off to pay for the extra miles as you go because your payoff will be reduced according to the vehicle's true value. If you purchase your leased vehicle at the end of the lease for the guaranteed or predetermined future value, you surely don't want to pay more than what it's worth. *This should be common sense.*

If you want to buy a more expensive vehicle than what your monthly budget will allow, then leasing can also be the solution. This can be accomplished with the longer-term leases. Yes, the longer-term leases, because most short-term leases are more expensive than conventional long-term financing.

Long term means 48 or 60 months and short term means 24 months. Long-term leases will reduce your payment and still provide a realistic residual value. Long-term leases are used most often on trucks because trucks have a longer life than cars. Trucks ($1/4$, $1/2$, $3/4$ ton and larger), also have a higher residual value. In a 48-month lease, the savings can be more than $150 per month—and you can buy it after 48 months and finance it for three to five years.

Now you have a 48-month lease and your choice of finance terms on the end. You could end up with payments from seven to nine years. An extended term is understandable, but try not to go longer than six years, anything longer and you're paying way too much interest. Pick a more modestly-priced vehicle if you have to rather than extending payments.

If the lease/purchase is an extended term, choose a vehicle that you really want. Also, make sure it's one that you won't be putting a great deal of miles on so that the vehicle will last. It's difficult making payments on a vehicle that's already worn out.

Leasing is your best option for short-term trading cycles and has its place for other applications as well. Sometimes the best lease program is the one advertised by the manufacturer or by the dealership. The best way to take advantage of it and not be maneuvered away from an advertised special is to follow the advertised guidelines *exactly*—meaning look at the cap reduction (the down payment), and follow it exactly. When you alter anything in the offering, you open yourself up to net cost changes that you would be unaware of. In other words, you could lose money because you as a consumer will have a difficult time figuring out the net cost changes and what the net cost changes should be.

Cap Cost Reductions

Leases will be advertised with a cap cost reduction. Cap cost is the capitalization cost of the lease, and when you pay a cap cost reduction it's a form of a down payment that reduces your payment amount. The down payment is subtracted from the usage fee you're paying and does not affect the residual portion of the vehicle, which is the amount of the vehicle you're not paying for. I'll try to illustrate it further with this example:

Example A		Example B
$28,000.00	M.S.R.P.	$28,000.00
26,000.00	Selling price	26,000.00
none	**Cap cost reduction**	**-2,000.00**
no reduction	Adjusted cap cost	$24,000.00
26,000.00	Capitalization cost	24,000.00
-18,000.00	Residual value	-18,000.00
$8,000.00	Vehicle usage amount	$6,000.00
$514.00	Monthly payment	$424.00

$$\$514.00 - 424.00 = \$90.00$$

Your payment is reduced by $90.00 because you're paying an additional $2,000 down.

If your cap cost reduction is $2,000, subtract $2,000 from the selling price of $26,000, changing your $8,000 pay down to only $6,000 because you've just prepaid $2,000.

I'll show you how it works, using the following payment factors will change your aggregate payment amount by more than $2,000 because you aren't paying interest on that $2,000. Using the following payment factors...

$45.00 per $1,000.00 on 24 months
$35.00 per $1,000.00 on 36 months
$32.00 per $1,000.00 on 48 months

...will enable you to determine the reduction in payment you will receive for every additional $1,000 you pay down to reduce your capitalization cost. Conversely, if you're looking at an advertised lease with a specified payment for 24 months, with a cap cost reduction of $3,000, and you wish to pay only a $1,000 cap cost reduction, your payment will increase by $90 per month because you increased the capitalization cost of the lease by $2,000. The payment factors can be used both ways.

Again, vehicle usage amount, lease pay down or depreciation amounts are all the same. This is the amount you pay the vehicle down. This amount does not reflect the interest you're paying. The interest you're paying reflects a declining balance from the selling price down because you're actually paying interest on the entire vehicle, not just on the portion you're paying off.

Advertised Lease Specials

The lease programs that are advertised are usually very competitive. Therefore, I suggest you take advantage of them as they are structured.

Let's say you're entering into an advertised lease special for 48 months. It includes a $2,000 cap reduction (to get to a payment of $392 as we have shown), and trading in a vehicle that's worth $8,000. In this case, you're best bet is to have the dealership take the $2,000 cap reduction from the $8,000 credit you're getting from your vehicle on trade-in and issue you a check for $6,000 (which would be for the balance of your equity). The other alternative is to use the factor of $32 and multiply it by six (which is $192), and subtract the $192 from the advertised lease payment to arrive at your payment. Thereby, you'll have used all of your equity to reduce the amount of your monthly lease payments.

Here's an example of a lease payment that's advertised with a $2,000 cap reduction:

$2,000.00	Cap reduction (as advertised)
$6,000.00	Additional cap reduction from your trade-in
$392.00	Payment (as advertised)
-192.00	(6 x 32 = $192 reduction in payment)
$200.00	Actual new payment

Be cautious if the dealer comes back with a new payment of, say, only $96 less than the $392. If so, then they just absorbed $3,000 of your extra $6,000 and converted it into their profit.

Here's another example:

$392.00   Advertised payment
  -96.00   Fictional reduced amount
$296.00   New payment offered

Be careful and remember that the best suggestion is to take the extra equity back in the form of a check.

Pre-Paid Lease

A pre-paid lease is exactly that: you pre-pay the entire lease and save money by doing it. Now, in order to really save money and not just make more profit for the dealership, proceed in the following manner.

Take the normal lease payments and multiply them by the term, such as:

$392 x 36 months =

After you have calculated the numbers, ask what the amount would be if you pre-pay the lease. Needless to say it should be less than the amount you're paying over the 36-month term. Usually, a pre-paid lease has a 2-3% smaller factor on the interest amounts—for example, 6% instead of 9%. The best

buys are when they are advertised. You should compare the total of the normal lease payments with the
pre-paid lease total to see what you're really saving.

My honest opinion of a pre-paid lease is not very
high, unless you can save a substantial amount. Avoid
a pre-paid lease without a substantial savings. A pre-
paid lease can also be a cash flow call on your part,
and can be used in your favor for tax purposes if you
need a lump sum to write off. If you're in a business
situation with the option to write off your vehicle, by
pre-paying you might be able to deduct the entire
amount in the year in which you make the payment
(check with your accountant regarding this).

Whatever you do, when entering into a pre-paid
lease, take the following steps:

- Have a normal lease figured.
- Compare it with the pre-paid lease numbers.
- If you have a trade-in and your trade-in is
  paid for, or has a substantial amount of
  equity, be careful that the dealership does not
  absorb your equity.

Again, you cannot receive a sales tax credit when
you trade in a vehicle on a lease because you pay sales
tax on your monthly lease payment, not on the entire

vehicle. This is also a reason why leases work as well as they do. As previously mentioned, one of the benefits in leasing a vehicle is that you pay sales tax on *only* the portion of the vehicle you pay for and you'll do it on a monthly basis—instead of paying sales tax on the entire vehicle.

Leasing is beneficial because it keeps you out of the used car business because you're paying only for the portion of the vehicle you actually use. If you don't want to own or drive a used car, then set yourself up by *leasing new vehicles.*

Used Vehicle Leases

There are also leases available on used vehicles, usually with a higher interest rate attached to them, so they don't pencil out quite as well as a new vehicle. You can usually lease a new vehicle for the same (in most cases less) as a used vehicle per month. In some cases, qualifying is easier on a used vehicle than on a new one, but all in all they are not as good a deal as a lease on a new vehicle. If you can avoid a used car lease, do so—unless they are available in the current year with low mileage. For example, it's 1997 and the 1997 models are available. You're looking to lease a used 1997. In this case, the interest rate attached to the lease for a 1997 used model will be the same as a new 1997 vehicle, so you won't be paying more for the same year vehicle.

Leasing "new" is more favorable for you than leasing "used." If you can only qualify for a $20,000 used vehicle lease and not for a $30,000 new vehicle lease, then you may have to accept the used vehicle lease. The new and used leases work the same way, meaning you pay the vehicle down from its present value to a predetermined future value. In the case of the $20,000 used vehicle, you would pay it down to $10,000 (hypothetically speaking), and then have the option to buy it for $10,000 at the end of your lease term.

Used business equipment leases have been available for several years. Used vehicle leases have only recently become available. Used vehicle leases have come into existence as the volume of new vehicles coming off leases by General Motors, Ford and Chrysler has increased. A used lease provides the manufacturers an additional way to market used vehicles.

A new or used lease works the same way. In a

lease, you pay for the portion of the vehicle you use, and decide later if you want to buy the rest of the vehicle. Just be careful to pay for only the portion of the vehicle that you use and not for the whole vehicle. A realistic profit should always be made by the dealer, but be astute enough to keep it realistic.

Remember, if you lease a car, you don't pay for the entire car. Instead, you only pay for about 50% of it, depending on the length of your lease.

Here's another point: When you use a lease to absorb a deficit of $2,000 (for example) on another car, your payments will change because you're paying 50% of the car's value and paying off the extra $2,000. This amount will be amortized over the life of the lease (24 months, 36 months, etc.). Consequently, your payments will be slightly higher.

Calculate this amount:

- $2,000 divided by 24 months plus the interest on the additional $2,000.

Or, simply use the money factor we spoke of earlier: On the 24-month lease at $45 per $1,000, this would increase your payment by $90 per month.

Ask yourself these questions: *Where did my deficit come from? Why do I owe more on my car than what it's worth?* There are a variety of possible answers.

1. You didn't keep it long enough on a 60-month finance plan. (You break even in the 49th month in a 60-month contract.)

2. You put little or no money down when you bought it.

3. You may have paid too much for it.

4. You may have financed it for too long.

As a potential lease customer, what type of lease should you look for? The answer is a simple straight lease, which we'll now discuss.

A Simple Straight Lease

A simple straight lease includes the following points:

- A guaranteed future value.
- The right to purchase a vehicle for the guaranteed future value.
- A designated amount of miles to be driven, (i.e., 12,000 miles per year or 15,000 per year).
- The right to walk away from the vehicle at lease end.

This type of lease will be referred to as a "Closed-end Lease." Conversely, never enter into a "Fair Market Value Lease," which is referred to as an "Open-end Lease." A Fair Market Value Lease gives the leasing company the latitude to change the buy-out price of the vehicle, and also gives the leasing company the right to charge you additional fees if the market value on your car goes below the expected future value.

Example:

Your Ford Taurus has a projected future value of $12,000, but at the end of the lease term the market changes and the value decreases to $10,000. In this case, a Fair Market Value Lease would give the leasing company the legal right to charge you the $2,000 difference at the end of the lease.

What they call the lease (an Open- or Closed-end Lease) is not as important as what the lease contains—so don't become confused with the titles.

What to Look For in Your Lease

Simply put, the shorter the lease, the better (i.e., two or three years). Never sign for a long-term lease unless you require extra time to amortize out a deficit on your current car. Short-term leases from manufacturers can carry lower interest rates. Car manufacturers want you to be in a different car as often as possible. Therefore, they make shorter leases more appealing to the public.

Remember, you pay for 40-50% (or whatever it works out to be) of the car you use, and you also pay interest. The interest you pay is a key factor because you pay the interest on the entire car. Ask what interest rate you're paying—good dealers will be glad to show you.

In summary, here's what to look for in a lease:
- A shorter term
- A good interest rate
- The ability to use it as a deficit reduction tool

One way to lower your lease payment is to put additional money down (see example page 24). In this example we discussed a trade-in with the value of $8,000. The $8,000 was additional down payment money (if you choose to utilize the entire $8,000 for a down payment). I don't recommend this. Leave your money in the bank and let it earn interest. You'll like the outcome and freedom of a lease more if you use the lease the way it's designed.

Negotiating a Lease

With a lease, you can negotiate the purchase price of the vehicle. It's just like buying a vehicle, except the manufacturers generally keep the rebates on leases because they are providing better lease interest rates. You typically cannot get both the rebate and the sevented (reduced) rate. Rates are sometimes referred to as "lease rates" or "lease factors," but the reality is both are in fact some form of interest rate.

Make certain you understand what the true interest rate is and not just what the lease factor is. A good dealer will tell you. If they won't, do business elsewhere or call your bank. Your bank can run lease calculations for you (many have leasing divisions).

In conclusion, you generally lease a car because you know a car will be an equity loser and not an equity gainer, so why put more than the minimum first payment and security deposit and license fees into it? Remember, cars *depreciate, not appreciate* (improve or increase) in value.

If you still feel leasing is not for you because you don't actually own your car on a lease, think about this: Why do banks have drive-up windows? Answer: *So the cars can visit their rightful owners periodically!*

Chapter 3: Should I Buy New or Used?

Sometimes you can buy a new car and your monthly payment is the same as a used car. Here's the reason: If you buy a used car, financing is usually available for two, three or four years, depending on the age of the vehicle. The older the car gets, the shorter term the bank will give you to finance it. In reality, you can buy a new car, spread the payments out for a full 60 months (as opposed to 36 months), and your payments will be the same.

There are two main benefits of buying a new car instead of a used car:

1. You don't have to pay the garage to keep a new car running.

2. A new vehicle has a longer life expectancy than a used one.

Buying Too Old of a Car

If you choose to buy a used vehicle, make sure the car will live longer than the time it takes to pay it off. I see people all the time who are trying to trade in a vehicle with 120,000 miles. High-mileage vehicles have no value left in them—other than a salvage value of $500. And even worse, customers often still owe $4,000 or more on them. In other words, stay away from vehicles that have space shuttle type miles on them.

Mistakes are made in purchasing vehicles by financing for too long a term. Let's say a vehicle has two years of life left in it. Based upon the miles you will drive it (usually 15,000 miles per year) and if you choose to buy it, do not *under any circumstances* finance it for a longer period than two years. Many people get into trouble by improper calculations and end up paying for a vehicle long after the vehicle is worn out. Such a situation can become a nightmare for four to five years.

You should buy the newest possible vehicle and finance it for the shortest term feasible. Here's reality: Most cars have a useful life of no more than 120,000 miles—and that's if they're serviced properly. At

80,000 miles, most cars are staring at some major service and repair bills, such as $500 to $2,500 "surprises." Such unpleasant surprises can be extremely difficult to fit into your budget. If you buy a used car, find one with less than 60,000 miles and plan on keeping it only three years. Make certain you do not finance it for more than three years or you'll be in trouble.

Older used cars are temporary fixes, so treat the financing on them accordingly. Trucks are a little different because they will usually outlive a car by a significant length of time. Trucks are simply made heavier and stronger. Another rule of thumb is the smaller the car, the shorter the life expectancy. This is a general rule (with some exceptions) because some smaller (including some subcompact) cars do last longer. Just be careful.

If you can buy an extended warranty on a used car, the car should be a safe buy. If the car no longer qualifies for an extended warranty, then you'd better be a mechanic or *walk away*. The nice thing about a new or newer vehicle is that you make only one payment on it per month, and typically don't have to make a second payment on it to the garage to keep it running.

My belief is either buy a new car that comes with a warranty, or buy a warranty for your used car. Usually you can finance the warranty along with the vehicle for an extra $30 per month. Thirty dollars per month is easier to deal with than a $1,000 surprise repair bill.

Buy-Backs

A buy-back car is typically a car that is a few months to a year old. Generally, this includes the current year vehicle which is being sold as new, or the previous year. You can usually get full-term financing for these vehicles. A buy-back car is a car that a large corporation had on a short-term rental, usually six to 12 months, or a car that was utilized by a rental company.

These cars are maintained very well and generally have between 12,000 to 20,000 miles on them. You can save a good portion of the original purchase price by allowing the first portion of the depreciation to go away. Consequently, a new car that costs $19,000 can generally be purchased in the form of a buy-back for around $14,000-16,000. This can result in a generous savings for somebody else just to break the car in.

If you purchase a buy-back car, there are limitations. Buy-backs generally come with one equipment package, usually one most of the public prefers. Be prepared to forego some of the options you may prefer. Many buy-back cars are not equipped with duel air bags yet and some minivans, for example, don't have seat beds. But other than that, typically the cars are going to be the same and have the same engine size.

An advantage of a buy-back car is that the balance of the factory's original warranty comes with the car. Depending on the manufacturer, most warranties are transferrable without additional fees. On the other hand, some manufacturers have a transfer fee—so you'll need to check into that as well. For example, Ford's newer warranties are on the vehicle, regardless of who owns it, up until it exceeds its mileage or time limit. The typical warranty is three years or 36,000 miles—whichever comes first.

Depending upon your situation and how new of a used car you purchase, purchasing a buy-back vehicle can be a better choice than buying a new vehicle.

The Next Step —
Questions To Ask Yourself

After you have established which vehicle you would like to own (new or used), the tricky part starts. You'll need to ask yourself these questions:

1. *What amount should I pay for it?*

2. *How do I know what I should pay for it?*

3. *How much time do I spend looking for the right price?* (Some people spend up to two months or more shopping price. *Hel-lloooo!*)

4. *Can I properly facilitate a transaction by going to only one dealer—thereby saving the time, energy, and money?*

5. *Do I dare say to the salesperson, "What's your bottom line?"*

6. *Do I/can I believe what the salesperson is telling me?*

7. *Is the salesperson going to truly help me, or is he/she there just to take my money?*

8. *Do I feel intimidated going into a dealership?* (Because you don't understand the car buying process and don't know what you should do.)

9. *Do I feel comfortable when the offer and counteroffer process is taking place?*

10. *Could I ever look forward to engaging in the car buying process? Would I have more confidence if I had more knowledge?*

Knowing the answers to these questions will make car buying a breeze. For example, if you have the knowledge, you will then be comfortable doing business at a dealership. This means you can then properly negotiate the right purchase price and understand the financing options available. After all, it makes no sense to get a fair price on the vehicle and then be taken advantage of with the financing.

Here's a very important point to consider: *You can hit a "home run" on the price, but the dealer can still hit a "grand slam" on your financing—whether you purchase or lease.*

Selling Your Current Vehicle Yourself

5

I f you have a vehicle to trade in, you can generally make a little more money if you sell it yourself, rather than trading it in. However, if you choose to sell it yourself, keep in mind the headaches that may come from doing so. You will find that selling a used automobile or truck is not always automatic, and when you weigh the time and energy it takes to do so, you may find it easier just to trade it at the dealership.

Understanding Book Values of Used Vehicles

You can establish a price for your trade with a simple call to your bank. Ask the bank what the book value is. Book value has three categories, and contrary to popular belief, they are not high, low and medium.

The book value categories are *average retail*, *wholesale* and *loan value*.

Average retail value. This is also known as

"high book" value. This amount is what dealers try to sell them for. Erroneously, people want and expect to receive retail for their trade-in. This simply isn't practical.

Average wholesale value. This is known as "low book" value and is what dealers will pay for the car. It's also the trade-in value. Unknowingly, people want and expect to BUY their new or used car at wholesale pricing. Again, *this simply isn't practical.*

Loan value. This is the amount banks will loan on the car, which is incidentally less than average wholesale or trade-in value.

When you sell your car on your own, you'll try to get a price which is about retail value, but your retail value will probably be less than a dealer's retail value. Most people are unable to make a vehicle look as good as dealers can, so you may have to accept a little less money. If you do choose to sell your car yourself, take it to a detail shop where they can enhance the car's appeal. Another reason you may need to accept less money is because you cannot offer a warranty like a dealer can.

In Appendix B I've included some April 1996 used car guide values from the N.A.D.A. Official Used Car Guide®. This book changes monthly, so make certain you access a current volume. Take a look at Appendix B now and familiarize yourself with the information found in the N.A.D.A. Official Used Car Guide®.

Trading Your Old Car to the Dealer

After you've found the car you want, you then have to establish the purchase price, as well as the value of the car you're trading in.

Example:

Let's say you're fed up with trying to sell the car on your own. When you trade your car to the dealer, you will want to get as much as possible for it. The dealer will pay you wholesale value. This is what you should expect. That's right, *wholesale*! If it needs new tires, take that into account also. If the miles on your car average out to be about 15,000 miles per year, then your miles are considered the normal average. If they are above average, this will also deduct from the value of the vehicle.

Note: There are high and low mileage charts within the N.A.D.A. Official Used Car Guide® (see Appendix B for reference).

Generally speaking, you should receive wholesale book value for your car, less $200 to clean and prepare your car for resale—unless of course you have some obvious mechanical problems, dents, poor tires, etc. If so, these items will devalue your car accordingly.

To establish what wholesale really is, ask to see the current used car book (the N.A.D.A. Official Used Car Guide®). Dealers use this book as a guideline. Incidentally, these are updated every 30 days and published by the N.A.D.A. Official Used Car Guide Company. By the way, this is the most commonly-used book—and *it's yellow, not blue!*

The other popular used car guide is the Kelley Blue Book. Different regions of the country will utilize either the N.A.D.A. Official Used Car Guide® or the Kelly Blue Book. Again, call your banker. He or she will know which is common for your given area. These books will have somewhat different suggested values, so make yourself aware of which is being used. You can usually find these books in your larger bookstores for purchase. They are usually published for the region of the country where you're living. If you live in the Pacific northwest, do not use a book issued for the southeastern portion of the country. Be sure to use the book issued for your region.

Here's an important issue: Don't think that if you go to five different dealers you'll find one willing to pay more for your car than it's worth. Dealers are all astute and work from the same books. They also go to the same auctions, and these auctions actually help establish the trade-in value of your car.

Now let's discuss cars that are soft in the market place. This refers to a vehicle (either a certain car or truck) that has a wholesale value considerably less than wholesale book value. The vehicle might be difficult to sell in a given geographical area, such as a sports car in a snowbelt region where it can only be driven six months of the year. In this case, your car will probably be worth less to a dealer than the book's suggested value.

Another reason vehicles can become soft is when there is an excess amount of a certain model available in the market place for resale. Another example on the other end of the spectrum is if a car is extremely unique, then the buyer is also unique to locate. Consequently, it will not sell fast from the dealership. If you have a unique car to sell, sell it on your own. If you have a Lamborgini to trade in, then a GMC or

Ford truck dealership is not going to appreciate it, nor do they want your trade-in. Dealerships will, however, check within the wholesale specialty car markets and try to obtain a bid from a sports car dealer or wholesaler who deals with specialty cars.

Upgrading used vehicles is another area that buyers get into trouble. Don't put too many improvements into used vehicles. Simply put: if you spend $3,000 on a new motor for a used vehicle, plan on keeping the vehicle for an extended period of time because that's the only way you'll get your money out of it. Dealerships can't give you what you've put into the vehicle because they will still be trying to resell an old vehicle. The consumer that looks at your old vehicle on a used car lot will simply not believe that the motor is new. Selling this is like saying the car was only driven on Sundays by a nice elderly person. *Helllloooo!!??* We both know that nobody believes that line.

If you modify your vehicle with a larger motor, lift kits, etc., plan on attracting a smaller market to buy it as well. When you modify vehicles, you're taking all the engineering efforts since the time of Henry Ford and throwing them out the window. I don't think it's a good idea. It might be fun but it can be hard on your car or truck, especially lift kits. This is just an opinion (and everyone has one, including me).

The auctions that dealers attend are really the heartbeat of what different vehicles are selling for in your geographical area. After all, if your dealer can buy 10 cars identical to your car at an auction, why would he/she pay you $500 or $1,000 more for your car? Sometimes a car can be as much as $3,000-5,000 soft in an area. Watch the newspapers and car lots to see what they are retailing for. This will give you some insight as well.

Sometimes you may feel the dealership is offering you way below a fair value for your trade-in. In some cases the dealer simply does not want your trade. He may have two or three units just like yours that he's had a difficult time selling, and he doesn't want to throw good money after bad. In this case, simply ask the dealer if this is the situation and try selling it on your own before you accept the reduced value from the dealer.

The only time a dealer will pay you a substantial amount more for your car is when he is charging you too much for the car he's selling you! I've actually had people go to another dealer and pay $2,000 more for an identical vehicle because the dealer was willing to pay them $1,000 more for their trade!

Figure it out: The person felt better because it was his trade-in at issue. *Don't become emotionally involved with your trade-in.* It's only nuts and bolts!

Here's a comparison example:

<u>A.</u>		<u>B.</u>
$24,000.00	Purchase price	$26,000.00
-<u>10,000.00</u>	Trade credit	-<u>11,000.00</u>
$14,000.00	Difference	$15,000.00

Needless to say, example "A" nets you a $1,000 better deal.

Establish a "difference" figure if you're going to compare prices. The "difference" means the comparison between the car you're buying and your trade-in. Remember, your car is worth wholesale value. Establish the selling price and then deduct the value of your car. Also take note if there is a lien on your car because *you* are responsible for paying it off.

Each transaction is based on the dealer's car

being "free and clear." Likewise for your car. The pay-off on your car is added to the transaction afterward and is included in the total amount financed. Keep this straight and keep it separate until the end. Hopefully your car will have a value that's greater than what's owed on it. You can find out by calling your bank before you go to the dealership. Ask what is owed on your vehicle and what the trade-in or whole-sale value is.

$24,000.00	Purchase price
-10,000.00	Trade credit
$14,000.00	Difference
857.50	6$^{1/4}$% tax
+150.00	License
$15,007.50	
+6,000.00	(Lien or pay off on your existing trade-in.)
$21,007.50	(Total amount to finance)

If your car is worth less than what is owed, you will have to make up the difference with additional down payment or add the deficit to the new purchase. Adding a deficit is a good way to get into financial trouble, especially the next time you trade, so use a down payment if possible.

Here's an example to help illustrate this point:

$24,000.00	Purchase price
-10,000.00	Trade credit/trade-in value
$14,000.00	Difference
857.50	$6^1/4\%$ tax
+150.00	License
$15,007.50	
+11,000.00	(Lien or pay off on your existing trade-in, which is greater than its trade-in value.)
$26,007.50	Total to finance

This scenario will mandate an additional down payment of $4,000 to bring it in line with the loan value on the new car of $22,000.

$26,007.50	Total to finance
-4,000.00	Down payment
$22,007.50	(New total to finance)

Some dealerships have programs with banks which will allow you to borrow more than the loan value on your new vehicle. This will allow you to include additional money you may still owe on your trade-in vehicle as a result of owing more money on it than it's worth (i.e., its deficit).

This problem can multiply because as you continue to trade vehicles your deficit will grow. Sooner or later you will need to get rid of this deficit. You must be aware of what's taking place with your transactions. You may be very well established and have great credit, and the banks may keep approving your vehicle loans. However, eventually you'll encounter a very large deficit (and have to pay the piper).

Generally, you can remedy the deficit situation with a lease. Leases can be very beneficial and help you in financing a deficit of typically $1,000-2,000 on your original trade-in vehicle. (A deficit is the amount you owe above and beyond what the vehicle is worth.) If you're short of cash, the lease will get you out of the deficit during the lease term. This is because the deficit amount is added directly to the amount you are paying the new vehicle down. This deficit amount is amortized throughout the length of your lease and will have no affect on the lease-end value or lease buy out option. At the end of the lease term you'll have cured the deficit created by the original car you are now trading in.

Your alternative in curing the deficit is to simply write a check for the additional amount you owe.

Example:

$20,000.00	(M.S.R.P.)
500.00	Rebate (if applicable)
-1,800.00	Discount (if obtained, including package discount on the window sticker)
$17,700.00	Adjusted price
+2,000.00	Deficit from old car amount you owe, more than it's worth)
$19,700.00	Total amount financed
	(Add license and document fees)

You can usually buy a car for less money than the window sticker price, and on a lease plan you can figure a discount as well—which we'll now discuss in the following chapter.

Chapter 7: Negotiating the Purchase Price

7

Before you even start negotiating a purchase price, make sure you're up front with the salesperson regarding when you intend to (or are able to) purchase a vehicle. Make sure you don't mislead the salesperson and waste your time and his/her time.

Here's a sample dialogue:

SALESPERSON: Tim, do you like this car?

TIM: Well, yes, I do.

SALESPERSON: If we can get together on a price that's suitable for you, when will you want to take delivery?

TIM: Probably in about two weeks.

Be honest with the salesperson. Let him or her know when you want the car. Furthermore, when you arrive at the dealership and first meet your salesperson, let him or her know when you need your vehicle. If it's six months, say so. If it's today, also tell the salesperson that. Don't feel you're giving anything away by saying, "Yes, I'd like it today" or "I'd like it in two days" or one week, etc. If you're up front about it, you'll get the kind of treatment you're looking for.

If you know you can't financially afford a purchase for six months, tell the salesperson that. Also, you may want to suggest that you're there to get ideas. If you're straight with the salesperson, he or she will better know how to effectively help you.

Establishing the Purchase Price

In negotiating the purchase price, you have to establish in your mind what you want to pay for your car. How do you do that? It's simple:

- Establish what the rebates are. Know how much and how many. You can find this out from the dealer because you, the buyer, must sign the rebates in order for the dealer to get credit for them when they are turned in to the manufacturer.

- What profit do you think the dealer should make? Contrary to some popular belief, a dealer does not have the large margins to work with that we have been led to believe.

Mark Up

What can you expect mark up on a vehicle to be? The amount of mark up on vehicles will vary. A good "rule of thumb" to use on a $10,000 car is $500 to $700. Here are some typical mark ups:

- Small to medium domestic cars: 6-10%

- Larger vehicles: 8-11%

- Trucks are 11-13% (larger trucks)

Also, remember to figure in the rebates as well. Rebates are for your benefit—so make certain they become part of the equation on your purchase. Rebates will also vary throughout the year.

The mark up on specialty and import cars is usually about 20%. However, these mark ups are also dropping. Depending on supply and demand, you will pay full window price for these if they are limited editions. However, you can typically strike a bargain if you go about it right.

How will you know if you're getting the correct percentage of discount on the mark up? Ask for it! A lot of vehicles selling for $20,000-25,000 have a mark up of only 9% to 10%. If you get a 5% discount and the dealer keeps 5%, that should be agreeable for both parties. *If you can split the mark up on vehicles with the dealer, you're doing just fine.*

If you want to purchase a vehicle for $500-600 above dealer invoice, offer that. You might want to offer it in writing. Such an offer will get the dealer's attention. This amount will work on vehicles in the $12,000 to $13,000 range, but on larger ones you're better off splitting the mark up because dealers can't afford to sell them for $500-600 over dealer invoice.

Dealer Invoices

Invoices vary from manufacturer to manufacturer. Invoices also show a dealer advertising fund, dealer interest payment and dealer hold-back fund. Remember, these items have nothing to do with the salesperson or sales manager. They have no control over these items, so your transaction has to be figured out after these items. Your split mark up starts after the invoice price.

Here are some suggested car buying techniques:

- If you go to any dealer and offer an unrealistic offer, you will not be successful. If your offer is sensible, they will either take it or make you a counteroffer.

- Always convey the attitude that you want a fair deal. Never convey the attitude that you want the cheapest deal. Everyone needs to win—you as the consumer as well as the salesperson and dealership.

- NEVER SAY: "What's your bottom line?" Instead, ALWAYS SAY, "I'd like to buy this if the price is agreeable." Or you can say, "I'm shopping, but I'd rather not keep looking if we can do business here."

A little car buying etiquette goes a long way.

Here's the secret: *If YOU and the DEALERSHIP can DO BUSINESS!*

When you get down to making an offer, indicate what you want for your trade-in at the same time. If you have a trade-in, make your offer $500 more than what you really want for the car. This option will leave you some movement, some negotiating room, as well as the latitude to do it. For example, if you want $6,000 for your car, start at $6,500. Then you have $500 to move. It's a good idea to move in $250 increments.

The purchase price of a new car is easier to establish. Generally, WHEN YOU MAKE AN OFFER IN WRITING (WHICH IS THE AMOUNT OVER THE INVOICE COST YOU WISH TO PAY), OR OFFER TO SPLIT THE MARK UPS, YOU WILL AUTOMATICALLY BE WITHIN $200 TO $400 OF BUYING YOUR NEW CAR.

Dealers rarely take your first offer because they are testing you, so don't take their first offer either! Instead, *test them!*

After you've purchased your car and feel confident in your salesperson, stay with that person. Let him or her assist you with all your automobile purchases. Here's where a little loyalty breeds loyalty.

If you don't have a trade-in, go into a dealership and create a win/win situation by saying, "I just want the price," and add, "I don't want to buy some other place. I want to buy it here, so please assist me in making my buying decision."

You know you can go to five different dealerships and get five different prices, but who needs the aggravation? All five dealers will give you about the same price, give or take $200 on a small car and maybe $400 on a larger car.

Use the invoice approach, use the dollar amount over invoice approach, or the split mark up over invoice. And use your banker to find out the value of your trade-in.

Here are the steps in figuring what you'll be paying for a vehicle:

- Determine the price
- Determine the value of your trade
- Subtract the trade from the purchase price
- Add tax
- Add document fees
- Add license plate fees
- Determine the total
- Add your old payoff (if you have one)

What Does a Dealership Expect to Make?

On small cars, the dealership needs to make $500 over invoice and hold-back fund (a fund that the dealer receives typically at year end and is utilized by different dealerships in various manners). Your actual transaction and the mark up on the vehicles I'm speaking of starts after the hold back fund, the interest (flooring cost), and the advertising fund. The actual advertising fund is a regional fund utilized by the dealerships in your region, which may be 10-15 dealerships (hypothetically) on various television promotions, as well as other media forms promoting the product.

On larger vehicles, they need to make 50% of the mark up between invoice and M.S.R.P. On the other hand, to get some vehicles (vehicles with a limited allocation), they will sometimes need to sell them for full Manufacturer's Suggest Retail Price, less the package discount provided by the manufacturer (which can be found on the window sticker).

Now most salespeople are paid 25% of what the dealership makes—and their commission starts above and beyond the advertising fund, flooring cost and dealer hold-back fund. That's not a great deal, considering the average salesperson sells between 11 and 12 cars a month. Typically, when you figure out what you're going to allow the dealership to make on you, figure that the salesperson is making 25% of that, which nets out about 20% because of the advertising, flooring cost and hold-back fund. Be fair with your salesperson. He's the one walking you through the process and he's the one who shows you how your vehicle works.

Your salesperson also becomes the liaison between you and the service department for the time you own your vehicle, should you have any problems. That's part of what he earns when you buy a vehicle from him. He not only gets paid for today, but gets paid for helping you with future problems. If you've been treated well, use that salesperson again. This is called "repeat clientele" by salespeople, and it benefits the salesperson and the customer.

Keep in mind that regardless of the vehicle size, each time a dealership sells a car, it costs them $400-500 in hard costs before they sell the car. That includes preparation, management and overhead. Dealerships have costs that must be met. If you understand this, you should feel better about the whole picture.

The Offer and Counteroffer

This process exists because the old fashion art of horse trading is alive and well, around the world, in Amcrica and in most of us. Your goal is to buy a vehicle and get a realistic price. The dealership's goal is to sell you a vehicle and make a profit.

Dealers want to work with you, but they don't want to just educate you for the next dealership. That's why the offer and counteroffer process works, it really gets you into the buying mode. When you make an offer, you psychologically are buying it. Just like the old cliché, you're now just establishing price.

I don't use an offer and counteroffer process. I prefer giving my customers a fair discount and doing the math for them, including figuring their payments. Most dealerships function with the offer and counteroffer process because it works. It's the old back and forth to the manager process that some consumers have learned to hate, but dealers use it because most salespeople are not capable of structuring a transaction and conveying the information to the customer.

When the back and forth process is used, the sales manager is responsible for structuring the deal, doing the math, and henceforth making sure he doesn't give the store away. Keep in mind that your new salespeople in the business will be trained in product knowledge, but in many cases won't have a clue to the financial end of things. Consequently, there is no feasible way for them to structure the transaction because they cannot figure it out. (No offense intended.)

Many salespeople who have been in the industry for 15, 20 or 25 years would still rather have the sales desk figure the transaction because it's safe and more often accurate. After all, the salesperson can still remain the good guy and keep the rapport with the customer. I learned the hard way that most salespeople would rather not change this process. I once challenged 15 salespeople to try my process, and two of the 15 were able to become comfortable with this process—the other 13 absolutely hated it and could not deal with it.

Salespeople who can work the entire process are hard to find. If you find one as a consumer, keep them and buy from them. You'll enjoy this short cut process much more than the back and forth process.

I have customers asking me the following questions: "See if they'll take this," or "See if they'll do that." They are surprised when I tell them that my process is different and I don't use a higher authority. Sometimes they actually feel a little gypped because I take the fight out of the process. *Go figure*—I guess it's just human nature and what people have become accustomed to. Yet most seem to really enjoy the process that I use. However, I've learned that if I shoot straight with people, they will usually feel oblig-ated to shoot straight with me—*and this will make the car buying process go much smoother for both par-ties.*

A good salesperson will be able to identify a real customer and a good, astute customer will be able to recognize a fair and straight forward salesperson.

If you do end up in the old back and forth process, never take their first offer—maybe the second or the third, but *never* the first. If you're in the process, just be patient and don't get nervous because your price will come to you. You'll know it when the movement in price is done in small increments.

Try an Alternate Strategy

What happens if a dealer won't deal right then and there? Give them space. You can allow them to call you at a later time and take your offer.

For whatever reasons, some dealers will not be able to accommodate your price right then and there. Give them a chance to call you back. In other words, you can politely thank them and leave, suggesting they call you when they can either meet your terms or come closer to them.

By the way, all dealerships work on a monthly volume structure, from the ownership through the managers and the sales force. They are all mindful of this because their paychecks depend on volume. Because of this, you should know you can strike a good deal toward the end of the month. So don't be afraid to call them back at the end of the month.

You can save money if you watch for regional advertised specials sponsored by the manufacturers on specific vehicles at dealerships in your region. When they do this, they will announce a savings of up to $2,500 (hypothetically speaking). The total discount amount is typically the package discount (which we referred to on page 7) and rebate added together.

They may also be advertising a specific equipment package and coordinate this with a special allotment of vehicles for the dealership to coincide with this offer.

Chapter 8: Your Credit and Car Buying

8

When you go car shopping, DO NOT complete a credit application unless you really want to buy or lease a vehicle you have already chosen.

The problem is this: When a dealership runs your credit, it shows up the next day as an inquiry. In the following weeks or months you do it again and again. If an inquiry shows up on your credit, it may be looked at as a loan you applied for that was DECLINED. Yes, declined. If you make the rounds, all of a sudden you have 10-13 inquiries, which really translate into declines—even if there are only two or three. Don't do it until you're ready to make the purchase.

When you really decide to buy a car and your credit is run at the dealership (most dealerships are hooked up by computer to the credit bureaus TRW, Trans Union, Equifax, etc.), it looks as though you've just gone through a series of declines, and the dealer will be led to believe that there are further problems with your credit that aren't showing up. The net result is that you may lose the opportunity to get the best interest rate available. Furthermore, if I'm a banker and I think that four other bankers declined your loan, I surely don't want to approve it by putting my stamp of approval on something that no other bank wants. Get the point?

Here's some straight information about credit worthiness I feel could be valuable to you. I have had a great deal of customers who should have had this information earlier in life. The credit bureaus track your credit by the way you pay your bills. When you pay your bills to your creditors, they automatically report them and their timely or tardy manner. If a bill is due on the 5th of the month, pay it so the payment lands on the 5th or the 6th of the month. If you go to the 15th of the month, which is 10 days late, that will be the maximum you can allow yourself to become tardy. Go past 10 days and you're flirting with a 30-day "ding" on your credit report. Good credit means nothing late, EVER! No 30-day marks on your credit. And absolutely no 60- or 90-day marks either.

Yes, you can go through life and end up with 45 accounts and nothing ever late. That's what you should expect of yourself and nothing less. If you have good credit, you will know it. If you have poor credit, you will also know it. And if you have rotten credit, you will most assuredly know the challenges you could face in financing a vehicle—unless you're totally clueless.

Incidentally, if you ever file bankruptcy, the bankruptcy will stay on your credit for 10 years. Plus, you'll pay for it with higher interest rates in the long run—that's assuming you're able to get any credit at all. Stay away from ever filing bankruptcy because it's very hard to leave behind you.

I've had customers try to buy vehicles who had previously filed bankruptcy against $5,000 or $10,000 worth of debt. I've seen some who have paid more in attorncy's fees than the bankruptcy's original debt would have totaled. The attorney got paid, the creditors did not, and the customer was branded with a bankruptcy for 10 years. There are times when it might be necessary because of a medical catastrophe. If this is the case, the 10 years of getting past it is much easier. It's one thing to have to get out from under $200,000 worth of medical bills that you had no control over, but it's quite another to spend $5,000 to $25,000 utilizing plastic, and then using the bankruptcy courts to hide behind.

STAY AWAY FROM PERSONAL BANK-RUPTCY IF AT ALL POSSIBLE.

The other thing which can absolutely kill your credit is a repossession, even if it's voluntary. It's hard for a bank to envision you paying for anything after you have had a repossession. Again, extreme circumstances aside, *pay for your vehicle or other goods at all costs and avoid repossession.* A repossession is very difficult to outlive.

A good credit rating will give you the best interest rates available. Currently, the best rates are about 9%. Poor credit can mandate rates as high as 25-27%.

In summary: Purchase only that which you know you can pay for and make your payments on time. It's important to watch your debt to income ratio. If your bills total more than 35% of your income before taxes, pay some off before going further into debt. *Lean and light is the theme here.*

Chapter 9:
Financing

Financing is the most important detail associated with purchasing your vehicle because it can seriously alter your overall investment layout.

On some new automobiles you can finance almost 100% of the purchase price through manufacturers' specials utilizing rebates (if available) as the down payment. This applies to new vehicles, and typically the consumer needs to have very favorable credit.

Used vehicles mandate that you may borrow up to loan value and the difference is made up in the form of a down payment. (See Chapter 5 regarding "Understanding Book Values," page 43.)

Finance your vehicle for the shortest period possible. Most consumers utilize 36, 48 or 60 months financing. Needless to say, the longer you finance it the more interest you'll incur. You're financing a depreciating asset, so it's difficult to increase your equity position in a vehicle, especially if you finance it for longer than 36 months. If your ownership cycle (the length of time you wish to keep the auto) is longer than four years, you can extend the payment term longer. The best approach is to finance your vehicle for a period of time no longer than the time you want to own it—and shorter if possible.

If you use 10% as an interest rate and finance $20,000 for 60 months, you will pay $422 per month multiplied by 60 months, which will be $25,320—plus tax, license and down payment. At a $6^1/4$% tax rate, the tax will be $1,375, the license $150, and a down payment of $2,000 will give you a **total down payment** of $3,525.

$22,000.00	Purchase price
1,375.00	Taxes
+150.00	Licensing
$23,525.00	Total Price

If you finance $20,000 (as per the following example), you will pay an additional $5,320 in interest. Adding that amount to the initial purchase price, the total cost of purchasing your auto looks like this:

$23,525.00	Total price with tax and license
-3,525.00	**Total down payment**
$20,000.00	To finance at 10% (approximately)
$25,320.00	= Payments of $422 x 60
+3,525.00	**Total down payment**
$28,845.00	= Total cost of $22,000 vehicle

Expenses associated with financing, taxes, etc., are realized by subtracting the original purchase price from the total.

$28,845.00	Total
-22,000.00	Price
$6,845.00	Total expenses

This is reality. The key variable is the payment amount of $422 x 60 months at a 10% or 14% rate. At 14% the rate would produce a payment of $460 per month or $38 per month more than a 10% rate, which is $38 x 60 months, or an additional $2,280 expense. It's very important to read the interest rate in the contract and make certain you leave with a copy signed by you and the dealership. Do not sign a contract unless the interest is shown and written in. The rate should be approximately the same as the rate your banker quoted you. (Remember when you called the bank before you went to the dealership?)

You may choose additional after sale items, such as extended warranties, climate protective products, credit, life or disability insurance—and add these items to your loan. Needless to say, this will increase your overall expense and you will have to recalculate your payments based upon these additional items.

To establish your payments, simply use a factor of $21 per $1000 financed. This calculation is helpful if you don't have access to the right calculator to figure exact payments.

Example:

A $20,000 vehicle would be $21 x 20 = $420 per month.

If you add $1,500 to the amount you originally planned to finance, you would multiply 21 x 21.5, thereby changing your payment from $420 to $451.50. This 60-month factor is a good rule of thumb, keep it handy. The following table should be helpful to you:

24 months $45 per $1000 financed
36 months $31.50 per $1000 financed
48 months $25 per $1000 financed
60 months $21 per $1000 financed
72 months $19 per $1000 financed

(These factors reflect an interest rate of $9^1/_2$-10%.)

If you use the factors listed above and the math does not work out, be persistent, question the transaction and demand an explanation. There could be an honest mistake taking place which will be corrected, or there could be a lack of communication between the salesperson and the finance manager.

If the amount is incorrect and/or you don't understand how they are arriving at their figures, whatever you do, ***don't sign it.*** Leave the dealership without your new auto rather than being persuaded to sign an installment agreement which you do not completely understand.

In Chapter 6 I referred to keeping your trade payoff separate until after you have figured the trade difference, then adding tax and license. This is the only way to stay on top of what's going on.

I will lead you through another example. Let's say you're buying a car for a $23,000 agreed upon price. The list price of the car is $24,200. The dealer is giving you $10,000 for your trade against the $23,000 sale price (not against the list price of $24,200). You have a payoff on your existing car of $8,000, so you're one of the lucky few with $2,000 equity in your trade. Watch these steps carefully. If the dealer gives you $10,000 for your trade against the $24,200 list price— instead of against the $23,000 negotiated sale price— you have just lost $1,200 on your trade.

Let's compare these two transactions:

A.		B.
n/a	List price	$24,200.00
$23,000.00	Sale price	n/a
-10,000.00	Trade credit	-10,000.00
$13,000.00	**Difference**	**$14,200.00**
812.50	Taxes at 6^1/4%	887.00
+150.00	Licensing	+150.00
13,963.50	Total	15,238.00

Note: The trade credit you're receiving in both

examples is the same, only the **sale** **price** changes the **difference** **figure** (in this case, by $1,200 plus the extra tax on the $1,200).

Now the amount left to add to your total is your trade payoff of $8,000. We will now carry the totals forward and complete the transaction:

A.		B.
$13,963.50	Total	$15,238.00
+8,000.00	Payoff	+8,000.00
$21,963.50	Total to finance	$23,238.00

Be careful! Use the structure in example A when you're negotiating your purchase, and make certain the final paperwork reflects the same mathematical outcome as example A.

A quick way to find out the difference is to compare the figures. The **difference figure** ($13,000) is key here, and it should be consistent. The **difference figure** increased by $1,200 in example B. Therefore, it cannot be as good a deal as example A. Be careful.

If you're comparative shopping and a dealer tells you that your trade-in is worth $10,000, find out if the $10,000 for your trade-in is against list price or a discounted price. The example previously shown will now become a good road map to follow. The **difference figure** is really what you need to know to tell you how much you're spending.

Now we'll use the same example, except this time changing the trade credit from $10,000 in example A to $11,000 in example B. You'll notice example A will still be giving you the best price, even though you're getting an extra $1,000 for your trade-in in the new example B.

A.		B.
n/a	List price	$24,200.00
$23,000.00	Sale price	n/a
-10,000.00	Trade credit	-11,000.00
$13,000.00	**Difference**	**$13,200.00**
812.50	Taxes at $6^1/4$%	825.00
+150.00	Licensing	+150.00
$13,963.50	**Total**	**$14,175.00**
+8,000.00	Payoff	+8,000.00
$21,963.50	Total to finance	$22,175.00

Occasionally a dealer will tell you they are giving you more for your trade-in, but as shown in this example you're actually getting less.

Remember, *it's the difference figure that really counts and must be consistent to produce an accurate comparison.* **The difference figure is the amount you are *really* paying.** Don't allow the dealership to tell you one thing and have the contract reflect another.

Another trick that exists is when the final paperwork is done, the dealership may try to tell you your trade-in can only reflect a credit equal to what the payoff is. This would change your trade-in credit from the above $10,000 to $8,000.

Don't fall for it. Get an established sale price and an established trade credit—and don't allow the amounts to be altered. If they are, don't accept the transaction, and *leave the dealership immediately.*

One exception in which the dealership may have to alter these amounts is when they alter both the <u>sale price</u> and the <u>trade-in</u> price *equally*. **Then the difference is not altered.** This is sometimes done to show a larger trade-in value on your transaction.

If there is limited or no equity in your trade-in, it will look like the following example C. Compare it to example A:

A.		C.
$23,000.00	Sale price	$25,000.00
-10,000.00	Trade credit	-12,000.00
$13,000.00	Difference	$13,000.00
812.50	Taxes at $6^1/4\%$	812.50
+150.00	Licensing	+150.00
$13,963.50	Total	$13,963.50
+8,000.00	Payoff	+8,000.00
$21,963.50	Total to finance	$21,963.50

The sale price and trade credit were both increased by $2,000. The reason for this adjustment would be to reflect a better equity position in your trade, thereby giving the transaction the appearance that the customer is putting $4,000 of equity into the transaction, instead of $2,000. In some cases, this will motivate a lender or banker to approve financing on your transaction. Why? Because the equity position in the new vehicle now appears to be better, even though it isn't—only the <u>effort</u> to increase the equity has actually been increased.

I'm not endorsing this maneuver, but simply explaining how it works in case you ever encounter it. Sometimes things move quickly in a dealership, and it's important that you're able to dissect what is happening. Do not become victimized by someone's paper maneuvers and numbers games. They can pencil whip you so fast you'll never know what happened.

Vehicle Equity

What is vehicle equity? How does it work? How do the banks look at it?

Banks prefer to be in an equity position with all of their loans. Banks want you to owe only as much on a vehicle as the vehicle's wholesale value. The reason is if they have to repossess the vehicle, they want to be able to liquidate the vehicle rapidly. They don't want your loan payoff to be greater than what they can sell the vehicle for. The banks are not in the car business, they are in the lending business. Banks will send your vehicle to an auction to be liquidated as soon as possible to prevent any further potential losses. Vehicles are repossessed for reasons other than someone's credit becoming poor or delinquent.

Another possible repossession scenario is when the buyer dies without adequate life insurance coverage and their estate does not have the money to continue making payments. There are a multitude of reasons why banks obtain vehicles which have not been fully paid off and they need to protect their financial position accordingly.

Equity in a vehicle is somewhat of an intangible. Most consumers that finance vehicles rarely build up any equity in a vehicle primarily because of what has become the fashionable way to purchase—which is with a very small down payment. As a vehicle is paid down, the depreciation of the vehicle goes at a faster pace than the loan pay down. The longer the term of the loan, the worse the situation becomes.

If you finance a vehicle for 60 months and put $1,500 down at the time of purchase, your depreciation will out pace the loan pay down for approximately the first 48 months of ownership. Prior to reaching 48 months, you will usually owe more on your vehicle than what a dealer will give you on trade.

A problem arises when the consumer chooses to trade the vehicle off and they find out they have a deficit on their existing vehicle. The consumer then has to pay an additional two to three thousand dollars to complete the payoff—which is higher than their vehicle's value to a dealer. The cure for this is varied:

1) Keep your vehicle until it's paid off

2) Make a larger down payment on it when you purchase it

3) Sell it yourself to the public

4) Lease the new vehicle and add the deficit to the capitalization of the lease

5) Pay off the deficit when trading it in

I personally don't think that having a great deal of equity in a vehicle is a smart investment because a vehicle is a depreciating asset. It's going to cost you money to own a vehicle, and when it's paid off it's usually not worth very much because it's simply worn out or out dated. That's the harsh reality of it. The only contradiction to this theory is for secondary vehicles, or vehicles which you plan to use very little. In other words, if you're planning to put less than the average 15,000 a year on a vehicle, it will last longer.

A good example is when you buy a truck or other form of RV and use it only 5,000 miles per year. You may find yourself being able to keep it 20 years or more. If you drive your primary vehicle a small amount, I suggest you also keep it for a longer period of time. Why? Because you have not used it up and you'll have a difficult time getting the extra value that you have not used up. Typical wear and tear cost on most vehicles is 12¢ per mile.

For example, let's say you're looking at two 1993 Ford Explorers (or two 1993 Chevy Blazers) and the vehicles have the same equipment packages and engine types. The mileage on one Explorer is 45,000 and the mileage on the other Explorer is 35,000. You then use the formula of 12¢ per mile x 10,000 miles. This will tell you that the lower-miled vehicle will be worth $1,200 more than the higher-miled vehicle.

This is my opinion: If you buy a new car for $20,000 and five years later you have put only 30,000 miles on it, you have really used only $3,600 of the wear and tear value, and you're certainly not going to be able to get $16,400 for it whether you trade it in or sell it on your own.

If your vehicle is looked at as transportation,

keep it and drive it. Most cars will depreciate 65% to 70% in five years. Yes, your car will be worth more than this because of the lower miles, but it will still never be worth more than 50% of its original value. Considering you have used only $3,600 of the vehicle's wear and tear value, that's a far cry from $10,000—which is approximately what you could get for your car on a trade-in.

First-Time Buyer Programs

If you're getting ready to purchase your first car, have someone co-sign for it rather than paying the 18-20% (or higher) in interest. Another good piece of advice is to have a substantial down payment and buy a small car. This makes it easier for you to establish your credit and then build up from there. As with any credit building situation, you need to build up gradually.

Sometimes manufacturers have special first-time buyer programs with specific lump some credits or rebates, such as $300 or $500. Watch the advertisements and ask the dealer. In addition, manufacturers sometimes offer a $300-500 College Graduate Program. Typically, you must take advantage of programs such as these within six months before or after graduation.

Dealing With Your Bank

When calling your bank to see what the going interest rate is for car loans, it's a good idea to get a commitment from them for the rate they are selling. Your banker is there to make a profit, so don't be surprised if they raise or try to raise your rate. The idea is to get a committed rate to compare to the rate offered to you at the car dealership.

Note: You need to be informed if you deal directly with your banker, just as you need to be informed when you deal with the dealership. There aren't any benevolent institutions out there. It's simply the free enterprise system at work. Whatever additional profit can be made, they will try to make. It's their job, and loan officers at banks and credit unions are simply capitalists at work.

Let's now discuss checking the book value with your bank on your existing car which you plan to sell or trade to the dealership. Sometimes employees at lending institutions do not totally comprehend the automobile industry, or they may not comprehend the exact information you're trying to obtain. Make certain your banker knows you're going to specifically trade your vehicle into the dealer—if that's the value you're calling about.

OR...

Make certain your banker knows you're going to retail your vehicle (if that's what you're going to do). The difference between the average trade-in value and the average retail value is dramatically different. You, as a consumer, can very easily be confused or led astray if you have the wrong information.

Example: If your car has a trade-in value of $11,000, you need to know that so you don't sell it on your own for less money than what it's really worth. If the retail value is $13,000, that's what you're going to try and sell it for—not $11,000.

Now let's discuss loan value, the other value in the book. Loan value will be less than trade-in value. Yes! *Less than trade-in value.* This adds to the confusion because some consumers will try to buy your vehicle with no down payment and finance it through their bank. Sometimes their own bank will start the process by quoting to the buyer only the loan value of the car you're selling, so the buyer comes to you and expects you to sell the car to them for the loan value.

In this scenario, the retail value being $13,000 and the trade-in value being $11,000, the loan value is $10,000—and that's what your new found buyer wants to pay for it. Well, welcome to the car business! Good luck trying to convince the person that they are wrong and you really are not over charging them. This happens everyday, and it all starts with incorrect information.

The structure of the industry is as follows: Loan values exist so the lending institutions are always in an equity position with their outstanding vehicle loans. Therefore, on loans that may go bad, banks can repossess the vehicles, sell them at auctions and typically get loan value (or close to it) out of the proceeds (or the price it brings at the auction).

Remember, loan value is less than trade-in value, so dealers will buy these vehicles at loan value or trade-in value. Usually the bank will still lose money when a car loan goes bad, but the existing system keeps it to a minimum.

The reality is this: You'll pay more than loan

value for a vehicle and more than trade-in value—and usually average retail value. If you're financing the vehicle, you will be making a down payment on the vehicle to close or lessen the gap between the **LOAN VALUE** and the **RETAIL VALUE** that you're paying.

Your credit worthiness and credit history will have an affect on how much the down payment is. Your down payment can vary from 5-25% down—possibly up to 50% down if you have not met your past credit obligations. And yes, some people will be declined all together because of their previous credit, or for having insufficient credit experience.

Debt to Income

Debt to income is important without saying because lenders do take this information into account. If you want to determine the amount of your auto payment, use $21 per $1,000 financed to get you close.

The formula will be for a five-year loan at approximately 10%, so if you're financing $10,000, your payment will be approximately $210 a month. At $20,000, the payment will be approximately $420 a month, and so on.

If you're looking at a $30,000 vehicle, do a little quick math so you're not surprised. If you calculate this before going to the dealership, it may prevent you from going into shock when the salesperson tells you the payment is $630 a month—when you've been expecting $350 to $400 a month. It will also be a quick acid test at the dealership to make certain they are not trying to retire on your transaction.

Chapter 10: The Business Office

10

Who is this person in the dealership business office? What services do these people provide?

That "person" in the business office does the final paperwork. He provides you with the interest rate, sells you additional warranties, and life and accident insurance. He also sells you after-market protection systems for your vehicle to keep it from rusting and to maintain its beauty.

What should you pay for an interest rate at the dealership? What should you pay for one-stop shopping?

Dealerships usually don't lend their own money. They will do your loan through either the manufacturer or through a bank. The dealership simply does the paperwork for the lending institutions. You will receive your actual payment book from the bank that carries your loan.

If you have your own bank, check with them before going to buy. See what the current auto rates are as they tend to change from year to year and will go up and down, fluctuating with the prime interest rate. Simply make yourself aware of the interest rate by making that simple phone call to your banker. Compare the bank rate with the rate the business manager offers. If the bank can only save you $1/2$-$3/4$%, it might be easier to take the rate at the dealership. Dealerships will often give you a better rate than what the bank offers. *This may be hard to believe, **but it happens**!*

Ask the business manager what his buy rate from the lending institution is. You can allow him to make $1/2$%-1% profit and not feel taken. After all, the business manager is providing a service also.

Chapter 11:
Warranties & Insurance

11

Should you buy a warranty? ***Definitely YES.*** If you decide to purchase a warranty, just don't pay too much for it. *Never drive a car that's off warranty.*

Warranties have different margins than automobiles do. I think a fair and equitable mark up on a warranty is $200-300. After all, warranties become worthwhile investments when you do need them, but never pay more than $1,050 for the "powertrain only warranty" they offer. If you choose an extended full-coverage warranty, you can spend up to $1,800. I feel that warranties are a must on used cars that no longer have a factory warranty on them.

Life Insurance & Disability Insurance

Should you buy the life insurance & disability insurance offered to you? If you're of the age and health to qualify for life and accident insurance, call your life insurance agent and get a quote. If you're of the age that you don't qualify through normal insurance channels, buy it! Insurance becomes a very personal decision—one that only you can answer. As with everything else, leaving behind an automobile that's paid for can be a benefit to your beneficiaries.

Chapter 12:
Summary

I f you use the principles and techniques taught in this book, eight out of 10 dealers will be happy to accommodate you.

Remember, if you leave a dealership and have to buy from one of their competitors, they have not made a penny. Their salesperson has struck out. You then have to travel to another dealer and start all over again. Remember, the dealership is interested in a win/win situation, so they will do whatever they can to obtain your business.

After reading this book and/or watching my tape, *How To Buy A Car Or Truck And Not Get Ripped Off,* you should now have the knowledge to understand them, their objectives, and be able to negotiate a fair price for yourself.

In summary, make sure you take care of the following:

BEFORE You Go to a Dealership

- ◆ Ask your bank how much you owe on your current car.

- ◆ Ask your bank what the current rate of interest is on car loans.

- ◆ Ask your bank about the "average retail," "average wholesale," and "loan value" on your old car.

- ◆ If you choose to do pricing homework on the internet or from price guides, do this before going to the dealership.

- ◆ Decide WHEN you want to buy. (Today? Two weeks?)

- ◆ Take a pencil, notebook and maybe even a calculator with you to figure your own math!

- ◆ Take this book with you as well!

While You're at the Dealership

- ◆ Ask how much you'll get for a trade-in on your old car.

- ◆ Ask about the price range of vehicles you would like to consider.

- ◆ Ask if there is a rebate on certain models.

- Ask what options are available on the kind of car you're considering (air bags, anti-lock brakes, warranties, etc.)

- Ask the salesperson about getting a new, used or a "buy-back" car. Ask about advantages and disadvantages of each.

- Select a vehicle.

- Agree on the price.

- Agree on your trade-in value.

- Have the dealership or salesperson figure your payments on a lease or purchase.

- If you're not comfortable with the outcome of the numbers, you can always postpone the final transaction.

- If you're satisfied, make the purchase and drive your new car home.

It truly <u>can</u> be this easy! As a result of using this book, you'll have a better understanding of how dealerships function—which will make car buying and leasing easy, painless and worthwhile for you.

◆ ◆ ◆

Appendix A

Residual Value Guide Examples
for Leasing

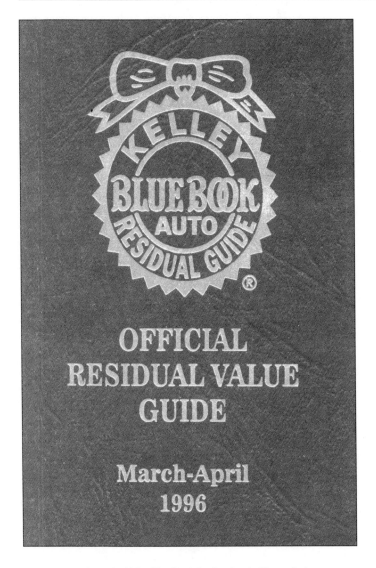

ORDER YOUR BLUE BOOK NOW!

Kelley Blue Book
P.O. Box 19691
Irvine, California 92713

Please accept our order for the following subscriptions:

Qty.
_____ Residual Value Guide
_____ Used Car Guide
_____ Older Car Guide
_____ Early Model Car Guide
_____ Advance Sheet
_____ New Car Price Manual
_____ Motorcycle Guide
_____ Motor Home Guide
_____ Travel Trailer Guide
_____ Manufactured Housing Guide

Send information on your personal computer products:

☐ POWERSYSTEM (new cars)
☐ KARPOWER (used cars)

COMPANY NAME _____

YOUR NAME _____

ADDRESS _____

CITY _____

STATE _____ ZIP _____

PHONE (_____)_____

Are you currently subscribing to any other Kelley Blue Book publications?   ☐ Yes   ☐ No

Check Enclosed ☐   Bill Me ☐
New ☐   Renewal ☐   Additional ☐

Phone in Your Order for Faster Service
(800) BLUE-BOOK or (800) 258-3266
(714) 770-7704 (So. Calif. & Outside U.S.)
(714) 837-1904 (Fax)

2

1996 AUDI

Body Type	VIN	List	Projected Residual Values			
			24 Mo.	36 Mo.	48 Mo.	60 Mo.
Quattro AWD	G,J		**2%**	**2%**	**2%**	**1%**
CABRIOLET—V6						
Convertible 2D	AA88G	37275	**63%**	**55%**	**47%**	**39%**

BMW

3 SERIES—4-Cyl.						
318Ti Coupe 3D	CG732	26180	**63%**	**55%**	**45%**	**36%**
318i Sedan 4D	CD732	30120	**62%**	**55%**	**47%**	**38%**
318is Coupe 2D	BE732	30995	**63%**	**56%**	**48%**	**39%**
318i Convertible 2D	BH732	35745	**64%**	**57%**	**49%**	**40%**
w/o Leather			**0%**	**0%**	**0%**	**0%**
Manual Trans	5		**0%**	**0%**	**0%**	**0%**
3 SERIES—6-Cyl.						
328i Sedan 4D	CD432	36410	**62%**	**56%**	**48%**	**39%**
328is Coupe 2D	BG232	36500	**64%**	**58%**	**49%**	**41%**
328i Convertible 2D	BK732	42875	**64%**	**59%**	**53%**	**44%**
w/o Leather			**(1%)**	**(1%)**	**(1%)**	**(1%)**
Manual Trans	3,5		**0%**	**0%**	**0%**	**0%**
Z3—4-Cyl.						
Roadster 2D	CH732	31445	**70%**	**59%**	**54%**	**45%**
w/o Leather			**(2%)**	**(1%)**	**(1%)**	**(1%)**
Manual Trans			**0%**	**0%**	**0%**	**0%**
7 SERIES—V8						
740iL Sedan 4D	GJ832	63060	**61%**	**56%**	**49%**	**42%**
7 SERIES—V12						
750iL Sedan 4D	GK232	92630	**49%**	**44%**	**38%**	**32%**
8 SERIES—V8						
840Ci Coupe 2D	EF832	76670	**58%**	**53%**	**46%**	**38%**
8 SERIES—V12						
850Ci Coupe 2D	EG432	95460	**53%**	**49%**	**43%**	**36%**

BUICK

SKYLARK—4-Cyl.						
Custom Sedan 4D	NJ52T	15995	**50%**	**43%**	**36%**	**29%**
Custom Coupe 2D	NJ12T	15995	**49%**	**42%**	**35%**	**29%**
V6 3.1 Liter	M		**2%**	**1%**	**1%**	**1%**
CENTURY—V6						
Sedan 4D	AG55M	17870	**51%**	**43%**	**35%**	**28%**
Wagon 4D	AG85M	18675	**50%**	**43%**	**35%**	**28%**
4-Cyl. 2.2 Liter	4		**(4%)**	**(3%)**	**(3%)**	**(2%)**
REGAL—V6						
Custom Sedan 4D	WB52M	20280	**53%**	**45%**	**38%**	**30%**

6   NEW 1996 VEHICLES ONLY   0396

1996 BUICK

Body Type	VIN	List	Projected Residual Values			
			24 Mo.	36 Mo.	48 Mo.	60 Mo.
Custom Coupe 2D	WB12M	19985	51%	44%	36%	28%
Limited Sedan 4D	WD52K	21735	51%	44%	36%	29%
Gran Sport Sedan 4D	WF52K	22340	52%	45%	37%	30%
Gran Sport Coupe 2D	WF12K	21495	51%	43%	36%	29%
V6 3.8 Liter	K		1%	1%	1%	1%
LeSABRE—V6						
Custom Sedan 4D	HP52K	21970	53%	44%	36%	28%
Limited Sedan 4D	HR52K	25975	51%	43%	35%	28%
LeSABRE—V6 (1997)						
Custom Sedan 4D		22545	59%	50%	41%	33%
Limited Sedan 4D		26095	57%	49%	40%	33%
PARK AVENUE—V6						
Sedan 4D	CW52K	28845	55%	48%	40%	33%
PARK AVENUE—V6 Supercharged						
Ultra Sedan 4D	CU521	33460	52%	46%	39%	32%
ROADMASTER—V8						
Sedan 4D	BN52P	26150	53%	46%	38%	31%
Limited Sedan 4D	BT52P	28080	55%	47%	40%	32%
Estate Wagon 4D	BR82P	28165	56%	48%	41%	32%
RIVIERA—V6						
Coupe 2D	GD12K	31710	59%	48%	39%	30%
w/o Leather			(2%)	(1%)	(1%)	(1%)
w/o Moon Roof			(2%)	(2%)	(2%)	(2%)
V6 3.8L Supercharged	1		1%	1%	1%	1%

CADILLAC

Body Type	VIN	List	24 Mo.	36 Mo.	48 Mo.	60 Mo.
ELDORADO—V8						
Coupe 2D	EL12Y	40235	54%	46%	38%	30%
Touring Coupe 2D	ET129	43635	57%	49%	40%	32%
SEVILLE—V8						
SLS Sedan 4D	KS52Y	43635	53%	44%	37%	29%
STS Touring Sedan 4D	KD529	48135	55%	47%	39%	31%
DeVILLE—V8						
Sedan 4D	KD52Y	36635	53%	44%	36%	28%
Concours Sedan 4D	KF529	41135	53%	45%	38%	30%
FLEETWOOD—V8						
Sedan 4D	DW52P	37635	50%	41%	33%	26%

CHEVROLET

Body Type	VIN	List	24 Mo.	36 Mo.	48 Mo.	60 Mo.
CAVALIER—4-Cyl.						
Sedan 4D	JC524	12872	64%	55%	47%	38%
Coupe 2D	JC124	12672	63%	55%	46%	38%

NEW 1996 CARS

0396   **NEW 1996 VEHICLES ONLY**   **7**

1996 CHEVROLET

NEW 1996 CARS

Body Type	VIN	List	Projected Residual Values 24 Mo.	36 Mo.	48 Mo.	60 Mo.
LS Sedan 4D	JF524	13395	63%	55%	47%	38%
LS Convertible 2D	JF324	17995	64%	57%	49%	40%
Z24 Coupe 2D	JF12T	14695	64%	56%	48%	39%
Manual Trans			(3%)	(3%)	(3%)	(3%)
CORSICA—4-Cyl.						
Sedan 4D	LD554	14885	47%	40%	33%	26%
V6 3.1 Liter	M		2%	2%	1%	1%
BERETTA—4-Cyl.						
Coupe 2D	LV154	14545	50%	43%	36%	29%
Manual Trans			(4%)	(4%)	(3%)	(3%)
V6 3.1 Liter	M		2%	2%	1%	1%
BERETTA—V6						
Z26 Coupe 2D	LW15M	17190	50%	43%	36%	29%
LUMINA—V6						
Sedan 4D	WL52M	16895	54%	45%	37%	29%
LS Sedan 4D	WN52M	18595	55%	46%	38%	30%
V6 3.4 Liter	X		1%	1%	1%	1%
MONTE CARLO—V6						
LS Coupe 2D	WW12M	17795	54%	46%	38%	30%
Z34 Coupe 2D	WX12X	19995	54%	47%	39%	31%
CAMARO—V6						
Coupe 2D	FP22K	17180	56%	48%	40%	32%
Convertible 2D	FP32K	22565	56%	49%	42%	35%
RS Coupe 2D		18785	56%	47%	39%	32%
RS Convertible 2D		24015	58%	51%	44%	36%
Manual Trans			(3%)	(2%)	(2%)	(2%)
CAMARO—V8						
Z28 Coupe 2D	FP22P	20685	58%	50%	42%	34%
Z28 Convertible 2D	FP32P	25785	58%	51%	44%	36%
6-Spd Manual Trans			0%	0%	0%	0%
CAPRICE CLASSIC—V8						
Sedan 4D	BL52W	20495	50%	42%	34%	26%
Wagon 4D	BL82P	22995	55%	47%	39%	31%
V8 5.7 Liter	P		1%	1%	1%	1%
IMPALA SS—V8						
Sedan 4D	BL52P	24995	64%	59%	54%	45%
CORVETTE—V8						
Coupe 2D	YY22P	38400	57%	51%	44%	36%
Convertible 2D	YY32P	46235	56%	50%	43%	36%
6-Spd Manual Trans			1%	1%	0%	0%

8   NEW 1996 VEHICLES ONLY   0396

1996 CHRYSLER

Body Type	VIN	List	Projected Residual Values 24 Mo.	36 Mo.	48 Mo.	60 Mo.

CHRYSLER

SEBRING—4-Cyl.
LX Coupe 2D	U52Y	17659	58%	51%	44%	37%
JX Convertible 2D	L45H	19995	60%	53%	46%	38%
Manual Trans			(3%)	(3%)	(3%)	(3%)
V6 2.5 Liter	N		2%	1%	1%	1%

SEBRING—V6
LXi Coupe 2D	U62N	20685	59%	53%	46%	39%
JXi Convertible 2D	L55H	25210	60%	53%	46%	39%

CIRRUS—V6
LX Sedan 4D	J56X	18895	60%	52%	44%	36%
4-Cyl. 2.4 Liter			(3%)	(3%)	(2%)	(2%)

CONCORDE—V6
LX Sedan 4D	D56T	19995	58%	51%	43%	35%
V6 3.5 Liter	F		1%	1%	1%	1%

NEW YORKER—V6
Sedan 4D	C46F	27895	53%	47%	40%	33%

LHS—V6
Sedan 4D	C56F	30850	55%	48%	42%	35%

DODGE

NEON—4-Cyl.
Sedan 4D	S27C	10830	60%	52%	43%	34%
Coupe 2D	S21C	10330	62%	53%	45%	35%
Highline Sedan 4D	S47C	12000	57%	49%	42%	33%
Highline Coupe 2D	S41C	11800	57%	49%	42%	33%
Sport Sedan 4D	S67C	13200	56%	49%	41%	32%
Sport Coupe 2D	S61C	13000	55%	48%	40%	32%

AVENGER—4-Cyl.
Coupe 2D	U42B	16046	58%	51%	44%	37%
Manual Trans			(4%)	(4%)	(3%)	(3%)

AVENGER—V6
ES Coupe 2D	U52W	18656	56%	49%	43%	36%
Manual Trans			(3%)	(3%)	(3%)	(3%)
4-Cyl. 2.0 Liter	Y		(3%)	(3%)	(2%)	(2%)

STRATUS—4-Cyl.
Sedan 4D	J46C	15820	56%	47%	39%	31%
Manual Trans			(3%)	(3%)	(3%)	(3%)

STRATUS—V6
ES Sedan 4D	J56H	18720	60%	52%	44%	36%
Manual Trans			(3%)	(3%)	(3%)	(3%)

NEW 1996 CARS

1996 DODGE

NEW 1996 CARS

Body Type	VIN	List	Projected Residual Values 24 Mo.	36 Mo.	48 Mo.	60 Mo.
4-Cyl. 2.0L/2.4 Liter			(3%)	(3%)	(2%)	(2%)
INTREPID—V6						
Sedan 4D	D46T	18995	57%	49%	41%	33%
ES Sedan 4D	D56F	22810	56%	49%	42%	34%
V6 3.5 Liter	F		1%	1%	1%	1%
STEALTH—V6						
Hatchback 2D	M44H	24996	58%	50%	41%	32%
R/T Hatchback 2D	M64H	28290	55%	47%	39%	31%
STEALTH—V6 Turbo						
R/T Hatchback 2D	N64J	35988	56%	49%	42%	35%
w/o Leather			(1%)	(1%)	(1%)	(1%)
w/o Sun Roof			(1%)	(1%)	(1%)	(1%)
6-Spd Manual Trans			0%	0%	0%	0%

EAGLE

Body Type	VIN	List	24 Mo.	36 Mo.	48 Mo.	60 Mo.
SUMMIT—4-Cyl.						
DL Coupe 2D	A31A	10806	56%	48%	40%	32%
LX Sedan 4D	A56C	13253	51%	44%	37%	30%
ESi Sedan 4D	A46C	13869	53%	46%	39%	32%
ESi Coupe 2D	A41A	11689	55%	48%	40%	33%
DL Wagon 4D	B30C	15215	59%	52%	45%	37%
LX Wagon 4D	B50G	16272	59%	53%	46%	38%
AWD Wagon 4D	C60G	16909	60%	54%	46%	39%
VISION—V6						
ESi Sedan 4D	D56T	19795	54%	46%	39%	32%
TSi Sedan 4D	D66F	24385	51%	44%	37%	31%
V6 3.5 Liter	F		1%	1%	1%	1%
TALON—4-Cyl.						
Hatchback 2D		15954	56%	48%	40%	32%
ESi Hatchback 2D	K41E	17029	56%	49%	41%	33%
TALON—4-Cyl. Turbo						
TSi Hatchback 2D	K51F	20140	56%	49%	42%	34%
TSi AWD Hatchback 2D	L61F	21695	55%	49%	42%	34%

FORD

Body Type	VIN	List	24 Mo.	36 Mo.	48 Mo.	60 Mo.
ASPIRE—4-Cyl.						
Hatchback 3D	T05H	9400	51%	44%	36%	28%
Hatchback 5D	T06H	10015	51%	44%	36%	29%
ESCORT—4-Cyl.						
Hatchback 3D	P10J	10755	48%	40%	32%	24%
LX Sedan 4D	P13J	12105	50%	43%	35%	27%
LX Hatchback 3D	P11J	11550	51%	43%	36%	27%
LX Hatchback 5D	P14J	11935	51%	44%	36%	27%

10   NEW 1996 VEHICLES ONLY   0396

1996 FORD

Body Type	VIN	List	Projected Residual Values 24 Mo.	36 Mo.	48 Mo.	60 Mo.
LX Wagon 4D	P15J	12490	51%	43%	36%	27%
GT Hatchback 3D	P128	14040	53%	45%	37%	28%
ESCORT—4-Cyl. (1997)						
LX Sedan 4D			56%	49%	40%	33%
LX Wagon 5D			58%	50%	41%	33%
CONTOUR—4-Cyl.						
GL Sedan 4D	P653	15980	56%	48%	40%	32%
LX Sedan 4D	P663	16995	55%	47%	39%	32%
Manual Trans			(3%)	(3%)	(3%)	(3%)
V6 2.5 Liter	L		1%	1%	1%	1%
CONTOUR—V6						
SE Sedan 4D	P67L	18865	58%	50%	42%	34%
Manual Trans			(3%)	(3%)	(3%)	(3%)
MUSTANG—V6						
Coupe 2D	P404	17135	56%	47%	38%	30%
Convertible 2D	P444	23935	56%	49%	41%	34%
Manual Trans			(3%)	(2%)	(2%)	(2%)
MUSTANG—V8						
GT Coupe 2D	P42X	19565	56%	48%	40%	32%
GT Convertible 2D	P45X	26430	58%	50%	43%	35%
Cobra Coupe 2D	P42V	26645	64%	56%	47%	39%
Cobra Convertible 2D	P45V	29415	64%	59%	52%	43%
Manual Trans			0%	0%	0%	0%
PROBE—4-Cyl.						
SE Hatchback 3D	T20A	16240	49%	42%	35%	28%
Manual Trans			(4%)	(4%)	(3%)	(3%)
PROBE—V6						
GT Hatchback 3D	T22B	19545	49%	43%	36%	29%
Manual Trans			(3%)	(3%)	(3%)	(3%)
TAURUS—V6						
GL Sedan 4D	P52U	19150	56%	48%	40%	32%
GL Wagon 4D	P57U	20230	59%	51%	43%	35%
LX Sedan 4D	P53S	21680	57%	49%	41%	33%
LX Wagon 4D	P58S	22700	59%	51%	43%	34%
V6 3.0L Flexible Fuel			0%	0%	0%	0%
TAURUS—V8						
SHO Sedan 4D	P54N		53%	46%	40%	33%
THUNDERBIRD—V6						
LX Coupe 2D	P624	17995	54%	46%	38%	31%
V8 4.6 Liter	W		2%	2%	2%	2%
CROWN VICTORIA—V8						
Sedan 4D	P73W	22140	55%	47%	39%	31%
LX Sedan 4D	P74W	23895	54%	46%	38%	31%

1996 GEO

Body Type	VIN	List	Projected Residual Values 24 Mo.	36 Mo.	48 Mo.	60 Mo.

NEW 1996 CARS

GEO

METRO—3-Cyl.
Coupe 3D	MR226	8996	53%	45%	37%	29%
LSi Coupe 3D	MR226	9396	54%	46%	38%	30%
4-Cyl. 1.3 Liter	9		1%	1%	1%	1%

METRO—4-Cyl.
Sedan 4D	MR529	9946	57%	49%	41%	33%
LSi Sedan 4D	MR529	10346	57%	50%	41%	33%

PRIZM—4-Cyl.
Sedan 4D	SK526	13205	61%	54%	47%	39%
LSi Sedan 4D	SK526	13855	62%	55%	48%	40%

HONDA

CIVIC—4-Cyl.
CX Hatchback 3D	EH235	10360	64%	59%	51%	43%
DX Sedan 4D	EG854	12630	64%	59%	54%	47%
DX Coupe 2D	EJ212	12280	64%	59%	54%	48%
DX Hatchback 3D	EH236	11630	64%	59%	53%	44%
HX Coupe 2D		13480	64%	59%	54%	47%
LX Sedan 4D	EG855	13980	64%	59%	53%	45%
EX Sedan 4D	EH959	16660	64%	57%	50%	42%
EX Coupe 2D	EJ112	15330	64%	59%	54%	48%

del SOL—4-Cyl.
S Coupe 2D	EG114		60%	53%	46%	38%
Si Coupe 2D	EH616		58%	52%	45%	38%
VTEC Coupe 2D	EG217		58%	52%	45%	38%

ACCORD—4-Cyl.
DX Sedan 4D	CD562	16280	64%	57%	49%	41%
LX Sedan 4D	CD563	19270	64%	56%	48%	40%
LX Coupe 2D	CD723	19070	63%	55%	47%	39%
LX Wagon 5D	CE182	20170	64%	56%	48%	40%
EX Sedan 4D	CD565	21780	62%	54%	46%	38%
EX Coupe 2D	CD725	21580	61%	53%	45%	37%
EX Wagon 5D	CE189	22810	61%	53%	46%	38%
Manual Trans	1,5,7		(3%)	(3%)	(2%)	(2%
V6 2.7 Liter			2%	2%	2%	1%

PRELUDE—4-Cyl.
S Coupe 2D	BA814	20340	62%	55%	47%	39%
Si Coupe 2D	BB215	23035	61%	54%	47%	39%
VTEC Coupe 2D	BB117	26260	57%	50%	44%	36%

12   NEW 1996 VEHICLES ONLY   0396

1996 HYUNDAI

Body Type	VIN	List	Projected Residual Values			
			24 Mo.	36 Mo.	48 Mo.	60 Mo.

HYUNDAI

ACCENT—4-Cyl.
L Hatchback 3D	VD14N	8690	57%	49%	41%	32%
Hatchback 3D	VD14N	9200	57%	49%	41%	33%
Sedan 4D	VF14N	9700	58%	50%	42%	34%
GT Hatchback 3D			57%	50%	41%	33%

ELANTRA—4-Cyl.
Sedan 4D	JF23M		52%	46%	38%	30%
Wagon 5D			51%	45%	37%	30%
GLS Sedan 4D	JF33M		53%	46%	39%	31%
GLS Wagon 5D			51%	45%	38%	31%
Manual Trans			(4%)	(4%)	(4%)	(3%)

SONATA—4-Cyl.
Sedan 4D	CF14F	15204	53%	43%	34%	25%
GL Sedan 4D	CF24F	16104	52%	43%	34%	26%
Manual Trans			(3%)	(3%)	(3%)	(3%)
V6 3.0 Liter	T		2%	2%	2%	2%

SONATA—V6
GLS Sedan 4D	CF34T	18404	56%	47%	39%	30%

INFINITI

G20—4-Cyl.
Sedan 4D	CP01D	27630	52%	46%	39%	32%
w/o Leather			(2%)	(2%)	(1%)	(1%)
w/o Moon Roof			(2%)	(2%)	(2%)	(2%)
Manual Trans			(3%)	(2%)	(2%)	(2%)

I30—V6
Sedan 4D	CA21D	32000	55%	49%	42%	35%
w/o Leather			(2%)	(1%)	(1%)	(1%)
w/o Moon Roof			(2%)	(2%)	(2%)	(1%)
Manual Trans			(2%)	(2%)	(2%)	(2%)

J30—V6
Sedan 4D	AY21D	40400	54%	48%	41%	34%

Q45—V8
Sedan 4D	NG01D	54000	53%	48%	42%	36%

JAGUAR

XJ6—6-Cyl.
Sedan 4D	HX174	56900	56%	48%	41%	33%
Vanden Plas Sedan 4D	KX174	65000	52%	45%	38%	31%

NEW 1996 CARS

0396 **NEW 1996 VEHICLES ONLY** 13

NEW 1996 CARS

1996 JAGUAR

Body Type	VIN	List	Projected Residual Values 24 Mo.	36 Mo.	48 Mo.	60 Mo.
XJR—6-Cyl. Supercharged						
Sedan 4D	PX174	66850	55%	47%	40%	33%
XJS—6-Cyl.						
2+2 Convertible 2D	NX274	62150	56%	48%	40%	33%
XJ12—V12						
Sedan 4D	MX134	79950	48%	42%	36%	29%

KIA

SEPHIA—4-Cyl.						
RS Sedan 4D	FA121	9910	59%	51%	42%	34%
LS Sedan 4D	FA121	11110	59%	52%	43%	34%
GS Sedan 4D	FA121	12010	60%	53%	45%	36%

LEXUS

ES 300—V6						
Sedan 4D	BF12G	34895	64%	58%	50%	42%
w/o Leather			(1%)	(1%)	(1%)	(1%)
w/o Moon Roof			(2%)	(2%)	(1%)	(1%)
SC 300—6-Cyl.						
Sport Coupe 2D	CD32Z	47695	64%	59%	52%	45%
w/o Leather			(1%)	(1%)	(1%)	(1%)
w/o Moon Roof			(1%)	(1%)	(1%)	(1%)
Manual Trans			(1%)	(1%)	(1%)	(1%)
GS 300—6-Cyl.						
Sedan 4D	BD42S	48445	59%	53%	47%	40%
w/o Leather			(1%)	(1%)	(1%)	(1%)
w/o Moon Roof			(1%)	(1%)	(1%)	(1%)
SC 400—V8						
Sport Coupe 2D	CH32Y	53845	64%	59%	54%	46%
w/o Moon Roof			(1%)	(1%)	(1%)	(1%)
LS 400—V8						
Sedan 4D	BH33F	54445	63%	57%	50%	42%
w/o Moon Roof			(1%)	(1%)	(1%)	(1%)

LINCOLN

TOWN CAR—V8						
Executive Sedan 4D	LM81W	37550	48%	40%	33%	25%
Signature Sedan 4D	LM82W	39600	49%	41%	34%	26%
Cartier Sedan 4D	LM83W	42600	50%	42%	34%	27%
CONTINENTAL—V8						
Sedan 4D	LM97V	42440	53%	45%	38%	31%

14   NEW 1996 VEHICLES ONLY   0396

1996 ACURA TRUCKS

Body Type	VIN	List	Projected Residual Values 24 Mo.	36 Mo.	48 Mo.	60 Mo.

New 1996 Trucks & Vans

ACURA TRUCKS

SLX 4WD—V6

Body Type	VIN	List	24 Mo.	36 Mo.	48 Mo.	60 Mo.
Sport Utility 4D		34320	61%	57%	51%	43%

CHEVROLET TRUCKS

BLAZER 4WD—V6

Body Type	VIN	List	24 Mo.	36 Mo.	48 Mo.	60 Mo.
Sport Utility 2D	T18W	21694	64%	59%	54%	48%
Sport Utility 4D	T13W	23742	64%	59%	54%	49%
2WD	S		(4%)	(4%)	(4%)	(3%)
Manual Trans			(2%)	(2%)	(2%)	(2%)

TAHOE 4WD—V8

Body Type	VIN	List	24 Mo.	36 Mo.	48 Mo.	60 Mo.
Wagon 2D	K18R	26596	64%	59%	54%	47%
Wagon 4D	K13R	31079	69%	59%	54%	49%
2WD	C		(3%)	(3%)	(3%)	(2%)
V8 6.5L Turbo Diesel	S		2%	2%	2%	2%

SUBURBAN—V8

Body Type	VIN	List	24 Mo.	36 Mo.	48 Mo.	60 Mo.
1500 Wagon	C16R	26709	68%	59%	54%	49%
2500 Wagon	C26R	27942	68%	59%	54%	49%
w/o Third Seat			(2%)	(2%)	(2%)	(1%)
4WD	K		4%	3%	3%	3%
V8 454/7.4 Liter	J		2%	2%	1%	1%
V8 6.5L Turbo Diesel	F		3%	2%	2%	2%

LUMINA—V6

Body Type	VIN	List	24 Mo.	36 Mo.	48 Mo.	60 Mo.
Cargo Van	U06E	18415	47%	41%	34%	27%
Wagon	U06E	20435	52%	46%	40%	32%
5 Passenger			(3%)	(3%)	(3%)	(3%)

ASTRO—V6

Body Type	VIN	List	24 Mo.	36 Mo.	48 Mo.	60 Mo.
Extended Cargo Van	M19W	19152	51%	45%	39%	32%
Extended Wagon	M19W	19736	61%	54%	47%	39%
5 Passenger			(4%)	(3%)	(3%)	(3%)
AWD	L		3%	3%	2%	2%

EXPRESS—V8

Body Type	VIN	List	24 Mo.	36 Mo.	48 Mo.	60 Mo.
G1500 Cargo Van			54%	48%	41%	34%
G1500 Passenger Van			54%	48%	41%	34%
G2500 Cargo Van			54%	48%	41%	34%
G2500 Passenger Van			54%	48%	41%	34%
G3500 Cargo Van			53%	47%	40%	33%
G3500 Passenger Van			53%	47%	40%	33%
V6 4.3 Liter			(3%)	(3%)	(3%)	(2%)
V8 454/7.4 Liter			2%	2%	2%	2%

NEW '96 TRUCKS/VANS

0396   **NEW 1996 VEHICLES ONLY**   **25**

1996 CHEVROLET TRUCKS

NEW '96 TRUCKS/VANS

Body Type	VIN	List	Projected Residual Values 24 Mo.	36 Mo.	48 Mo.	60 Mo.
V8 6.5L Turbo Diesel			3%	3%	3%	2%
SPORTVAN—V8						
G30 Sportvan	G35K	23451	53%	46%	40%	33%
V8 454/7.4 Liter	N		2%	2%	2%	2%
V8 6.5 Liter Diesel	Y		(3%)	(3%)	(3%)	(3%)
G-SERIES—V6						
G30 Van	G35Z	19504	53%	47%	40%	33%
V8 5.7 Liter	K		2%	2%	2%	2%
V8 454/7.4 Liter	N		3%	3%	3%	2%
V8 6.5 Liter Diesel	Y		(4%)	(4%)	(3%)	(3%)
HI-CUBE—V8						
1 Van 10'	G31K		42%	37%	31%	25%
1 Van 12' DR	G31K		43%	38%	32%	26%
1 Van 14' DR	G31K		43%	38%	32%	27%
V8 454/7.4 Liter	N		2%	2%	2%	1%
V8 6.5 Liter Diesel	Y		(3%)	(3%)	(3%)	(2%)
STEP VAN—V6						
1 Van 10½' DR	P32Z		51%	45%	38%	30%
1 Van 12½' DR	P32Z		50%	44%	37%	30%
1 Van 14½' DR	P32Z		50%	45%	38%	31%
V8 5.7 Liter	K		2%	2%	2%	2%
V8 454/7.4 Liter	N		3%	3%	2%	2%
V8 6.5 Liter Diesel	Y		(4%)	(3%)	(3%)	(3%)
S10 PICKUP—4-Cyl.						
½ Short Bed	S144	11755	64%	57%	48%	39%
½ Long Bed	S144	12065	63%	56%	47%	38%
½ LS Short Bed	S144	12770	63%	56%	47%	38%
½ LS Long Bed	S144	13065	63%	56%	47%	38%
½ LS Extended Cab	S194	14470	64%	57%	49%	40%
4WD	T		4%	4%	4%	4%
V6 4.3 Liter	Z		3%	3%	3%	2%
V6 4.3L High Output	W		4%	4%	4%	3%
FULL SIZE PICKUP—V6						
1500 ½ W/T Short Bed	C14W	14131	54%	52%	47%	40%
1500 ½ W/T Long Bed	C14W	14531	53%	51%	46%	39%
4WD	K		4%	4%	4%	4%
FULL SIZE PICKUP—V8						
1500 ½ Short Bed	C14M	18311	63%	59%	54%	46%
1500 ½ Long Bed	C14M	18591	60%	57%	52%	44%
2500 ¾ Long Bed	C24M	19273	64%	59%	54%	48%
3500 1 Long Bed	C34R	20477	64%	59%	54%	46%
4WD	K		4%	4%	4%	4%
Manual Trans			(3%)	(2%)	(2%)	(2%)
V6 4.3 Liter	W		(3%)	(3%)	(3%)	(3%)
V8 5.7 Liter	R		1%	1%	1%	1%
V8 454/7.4 Liter	J		2%	2%	2%	2%

26   NEW 1996 VEHICLES ONLY   0396

1996 CHEVROLET TRUCKS

Body Type	VIN	List	Projected Residual Values 24 Mo.	36 Mo.	48 Mo.	60 Mo.
V8 6.5L Turbo Diesel	F,S	....	**3%**	**3%**	**3%**	**3%**
EXTENDED CAB PICKUP—V8						
1500 ½ Short Bed	C19M	20371	**64%**	**59%**	**54%**	**49%**
1500 ½ Long Bed	C19M	20819	**64%**	**59%**	**54%**	**48%**
2500 ¾ Short Bed	C29M	21889	**64%**	**59%**	**54%**	**49%**
2500 ¾ Long Bed	C29R	21946	**64%**	**59%**	**54%**	**48%**
3500 1 Long Bed	C39R	23903	**63%**	**59%**	**53%**	**45%**
4WD	K	....	**4%**	**4%**	**4%**	**3%**
Manual Trans		....	**(2%)**	**(2%)**	**(2%)**	**(2%)**
V6 4.3 Liter	W	....	**(3%)**	**(3%)**	**(3%)**	**(2%)**
V8 5.7 Liter	R	....	**1%**	**1%**	**1%**	**1%**
V8 454/7.4 Liter	J	....	**2%**	**2%**	**2%**	**2%**
V8 6.5L Turbo Diesel	F,S	....	**3%**	**3%**	**2%**	**2%**
CREW CAB PICKUP—V8						
3500 1 Long Bed	C33R	23611	**64%**	**59%**	**54%**	**45%**
4WD	K	....	**4%**	**4%**	**4%**	**3%**
Manual Trans		....	**(2%)**	**(2%)**	**(2%)**	**(2%)**
V8 454/7.4 Liter	J	....	**2%**	**2%**	**2%**	**2%**
V8 6.5L Turbo Diesel	F	....	**3%**	**3%**	**3%**	**2%**
CAB-CHASSIS—V8						
¾ Cab-Chassis	C24R	18116	**58%**	**55%**	**49%**	**42%**
1 Cab-Ch 131.5"	C34R	18255	**58%**	**55%**	**49%**	**41%**
1 Cab-Ch/DR 135.5"	C34R	19265	**59%**	**55%**	**50%**	**42%**
1 Cab-Ch/DR 159.5"	C34R	19419	**58%**	**55%**	**50%**	**42%**
1 Crew Cab-Chassis	C34R	20893	**61%**	**58%**	**52%**	**43%**
4WD	K	....	**4%**	**4%**	**4%**	**4%**
V8 454/7.4 Liter	J	....	**2%**	**2%**	**2%**	**2%**
V8 6.5L Turbo Diesel	F	....	**3%**	**3%**	**3%**	**3%**

CHRYSLER VAN

TOWN & COUNTRY—V6						
Wagon	P54R	25865	**64%**	**59%**	**53%**	**45%**
LX Wagon	P55R	25850	**64%**	**59%**	**54%**	**47%**
LXi Wagon	P64L	30605	**63%**	**58%**	**51%**	**43%**

DODGE TRUCKS

CARAVAN—V6						
Wagon	P25B	18510	**63%**	**56%**	**48%**	**40%**
SE Wagon	P45B	21070	**62%**	**55%**	**48%**	**40%**
LE Wagon	P55R	24180	**60%**	**54%**	**47%**	**39%**
ES Wagon	P55R	25605	**60%**	**53%**	**47%**	**39%**
Grand Wagon	P24B	19410	**64%**	**58%**	**51%**	**42%**
SE Grand Wagon	P44B	21810	**64%**	**58%**	**50%**	**42%**
LE Grand Wagon	P54R	24670	**62%**	**56%**	**49%**	**40%**
ES Grand Wagon	P54R	26595	**61%**	**55%**	**48%**	**40%**

NEW '96 TRUCKS/VANS

0396   **NEW 1996 VEHICLES ONLY**   **27**

1996 DODGE TRUCKS

Body Type	VIN	List	Projected Residual Values			
			24 Mo.	36 Mo.	48 Mo.	60 Mo.
4-Cyl. 2.4 Liter	X		(5%)	(4%)	(4%)	(4%)
RAM WAGON—V8						
1500 ½ Wagon	B15Y	19965	63%	56%	48%	40%
2500 ¾ Wagon	B25Y	21374	61%	54%	47%	39%
3500 1 Wagon	B35Y	22575	59%	52%	45%	38%
V6 3.9 Liter	X		(3%)	(3%)	(3%)	(2%)
V8 5.9 Liter	Z		0%	0%	0%	0%
RAM VAN—V6						
1500 ½ Van	B11X	18460	55%	49%	42%	34%
2500 ¾ Van	B21X	18563	55%	49%	42%	34%
V8 5.2L or 5.9 Liter	Y,Z		2%	2%	2%	1%
RAM VAN—V8						
3500 1 Van	B31Y	21075	52%	47%	40%	33%
V8 5.9 Liter	Z		0%	0%	0%	0%
DAKOTA PICKUP—4-Cyl.						
½ WS Short Bed	L26G	11764	57%	50%	41%	33%
½ WS Long Bed	L26G	12380	56%	49%	41%	32%
½ Sport Short Bed	L26G	12440	64%	56%	47%	37%
½ Short Bed	L26G	13665	59%	52%	43%	34%
½ Long Bed	L26G	14176	59%	52%	43%	34%
4WD	G		4%	4%	4%	4%
V6 3.9 Liter	X		2%	2%	2%	2%
V8 5.2 Liter	Y		3%	3%	2%	2%
DAKOTA PICKUP—V6						
½ Sport Club Cab	L23X	15616	64%	59%	54%	45%
½ Club Cab	L23X	16746	64%	58%	50%	41%
4WD	G		4%	4%	4%	4%
V8 5.2 Liter	Y		3%	2%	2%	2%
FULL SIZE PICKUP—V6						
1500 ½ WS Short Bed	C16X	14546	56%	54%	50%	43%
1500 ½ WS Long Bed	C16X	14818	53%	52%	48%	41%
FULL SIZE PICKUP—V8						
1500 ½ Short Bed	C16Y	18032	64%	59%	54%	48%
1500 ½ Long Bed	C16Y	18316	64%	59%	54%	47%
2500 ¾ Long Bed	C26Y	19569	64%	59%	54%	49%
3500 1 Long Bed	C36Z	22286	60%	57%	52%	43%
4WD	F		4%	4%	4%	3%
Manual Trans			(2%)	(2%)	(2%)	(2%)
V6 3.9 Liter	X		(3%)	(3%)	(3%)	(2%)
6-Cyl. 5.9L Turbo Dsl	C		4%	4%	4%	4%
V8 5.9 Liter	Z		1%	1%	1%	1%
V10 8.0 Liter	W		1%	1%	1%	1%
CLUB CAB PICKUP—V8						
1500 ½ Short Bed	C13Y	20190	64%	59%	54%	48%
1500 ½ Long Bed	C13Y	20471	64%	59%	54%	47%

28   NEW 1996 VEHICLES ONLY   0396

119

1996 DODGE TRUCKS

Body Type	VIN	List	Projected Residual Values			
			24 Mo.	36 Mo.	48 Mo.	60 Mo.
2500 ¾ Short Bed	C23Z	22958	64%	59%	54%	47%
2500 ¾ Long Bed	C23Z	23164	63%	59%	53%	45%
3500 1 Long Bed	C33Z	24685	62%	59%	53%	44%
4WD	F		4%	4%	3%	3%
Manual Trans			(2%)	(2%)	(2%)	(2%)
6-Cyl. 5.9L Turbo Dsl	C		4%	4%	4%	4%
V8 5.9 Liter	Z		1%	1%	1%	1%
V10 8.0 Liter	W		1%	1%	1%	1%
CAB-CHASSIS—V8						
2500 ¾ Cab-Chassis	C26Z	18813	58%	55%	49%	41%
3500 1 Cb-Ch/DR 139	C36Z	19755	58%	55%	49%	41%
3500 1 Cb-Ch/DR 163	C36Z	19910	58%	55%	49%	41%
4WD	F		4%	4%	4%	4%
6-Cyl. 5.9L Turbo Dsl	C		4%	4%	4%	4%
V10 8.0 Liter	W		2%	2%	1%	1%

FORD TRUCKS

Body Type	VIN	List	24 Mo.	36 Mo.	48 Mo.	60 Mo.
EXPLORER 4WD—V6						
Utility 2D	U24X	22980	59%	55%	49%	42%
Utility 4D	U34X	24335	62%	57%	52%	44%
2WD	2		(4%)	(4%)	(4%)	(3%)
AWD	5		0%	0%	0%	0%
Manual Trans			(2%)	(2%)	(2%)	(2%)
V8 5.0 Liter	P		1%	1%	1%	1%
BRONCO 4WD—V8						
Wagon 2D	U15N	25375	60%	55%	50%	42%
Manual Trans			(2%)	(2%)	(2%)	(2%)
V8 5.8 Liter	H		1%	1%	1%	1%
AEROSTAR—V6						
Cargo Van	A14U	17966	50%	44%	37%	30%
Wagon	A11U	18375	60%	54%	47%	38%
Extended Wagon	A31U	22840	53%	48%	41%	34%
5 Passenger			(3%)	(3%)	(3%)	(2%)
4WD	2,4		3%	2%	2%	2%
V6 4.0 Liter	X		1%	1%	1%	1%
WINDSTAR—V6						
Cargo Van	A544	18825	55%	49%	43%	35%
Wagon	A514	20785	60%	54%	47%	39%
CLUB WAGON—V8						
Wagon	E11N	22224	57%	50%	44%	36%
Super Wagon	S31H	25764	57%	50%	44%	37%
6-Cyl. 4.9 Liter	Y		(3%)	(3%)	(2%)	(2%)
V8 5.8 Liter	H		0%	0%	0%	0%
V8 460/7.5 Liter	G		2%	2%	2%	1%
V8 7.3L Turbo Diesel	F		3%	3%	2%	2%

NEW '96 TRUCKS/VANS

0396   **NEW 1996 VEHICLES ONLY   29**

1996 FORD TRUCKS

NEW '96 TRUCKS/VANS

Body Type	VIN	List	Projected Residual Values			
			24 Mo.	36 Mo.	48 Mo.	60 Mo.
ECONOLINE—6-Cyl.						
E150 ½ Van	E14Y	19346	54%	49%	41%	34%
E250 ¾ Van	E24Y	19771	53%	48%	41%	33%
E350 1 Van	E34Y	21396	50%	45%	38%	31%
V8 5.0L or 5.8 Liter	N,H		2%	2%	2%	2%
V8 460/7.5 Liter	G		3%	3%	2%	2%
V8 7.3L Turbo Diesel	F		4%	3%	3%	3%
E350 CUTAWAY VAN—V8						
E350 1 Ctwy 12'	E37H	18533	51%	46%	39%	32%
E350 1 Ctwy 14' DR	E37H	19348	50%	45%	38%	31%
E350 1 Ctwy 15' DR	E37H	19823	50%	45%	38%	31%
V8 460/7.5 Liter	G		2%	2%	2%	2%
V8 7.3L Turbo Diesel	F		4%	3%	3%	3%
RANGER PICKUP—4-Cyl.						
½ XL Short Bed	R10A	11087	61%	53%	45%	36%
½ XL Long Bed	R10A	11472	61%	53%	45%	36%
½ XL Super Cab	R14A	14217	59%	52%	44%	36%
½ Splash Short Bed	R10A	14645	63%	56%	48%	39%
½ Splash Super Cab	R14A	16305	63%	57%	49%	40%
4WD	1,5		4%	4%	4%	4%
V6 3.0 Liter	U		2%	2%	2%	1%
V6 4.0 Liter	X		3%	2%	2%	2%
FULL SIZE PICKUP—6-Cyl.						
F150 Special Short Bed	F15Y	14765	47%	46%	42%	36%
F150 Special Long Bed	F15Y	15035	46%	44%	41%	34%
4WD	4		4%	4%	4%	4%
V8 5.0 Liter	N		3%	2%	2%	2%
FULL SIZE PICKUP—V8						
F150 ½ Short Bed	F15N	18327	55%	53%	48%	41%
F150 ½ Long Bed	F15N	18552	55%	53%	48%	41%
F250 ¾ Long Bed	F25H	19017	62%	59%	53%	45%
F350 1 Long Bed	F35H	20157	60%	57%	51%	43%
4WD	4,6		4%	4%	4%	4%
Manual Trans			(3%)	(2%)	(2%)	(2%)
6-Cyl. 4.9 Liter	Y		(3%)	(3%)	(3%)	(3%)
V8 5.8 Liter	H		1%	1%	1%	1%
V8 460/7.5 Liter	G		2%	2%	2%	2%
V8 7.3L Turbo Diesel	F		4%	3%	3%	3%
FULL SIZE PICKUP—V8 (1997)						
F150 ½ Short Bed		17459	66%	65%	59%	53%
F150 ½ Long Bed		17729	65%	64%	58%	53%
4WD			4%	4%	4%	4%
Manual Trans			(3%)	(3%)	(3%)	(3%)
V6 4.2 Liter	2		(4%)	(4%)	(4%)	(3%)
V8 5.4 Liter			1%	1%	1%	1%

30   NEW 1996 VEHICLES ONLY   0396

1996 FORD TRUCKS

Body Type	VIN	List	Projected Residual Values			
			24 Mo.	36 Mo.	48 Mo.	60 Mo.
SUPER CAB PICKUP—6-Cyl.						
F150 Special Short Bed	X15Y	16385	**56%**	**53%**	**49%**	**41%**
F150 Special Long Bed	X15Y	16620	**55%**	**52%**	**47%**	**39%**
V8 5.0 Liter	N		**2%**	**2%**	**2%**	**2%**
SUPER CAB PICKUP—V8						
F150 ½ Short Bed	X15N	20352	**64%**	**59%**	**54%**	**45%**
F150 ½ Long Bed	X15N	20597	**63%**	**59%**	**53%**	**44%**
F250 ¾ Short Bed	X25H	21667	**61%**	**58%**	**52%**	**43%**
F250 ¾ Long Bed	X25H	21487	**62%**	**59%**	**53%**	**44%**
F350 1 Long Bed	X35G	23485	**58%**	**55%**	**49%**	**41%**
4WD	4,6		**4%**	**4%**	**4%**	**3%**
Manual Trans			**(2%)**	**(2%)**	**(2%)**	**(2%)**
6-Cyl. 4.9 Liter	Y		**(3%)**	**(3%)**	**(3%)**	**(2%)**
V8 5.8 Liter	H		**1%**	**1%**	**1%**	**1%**
V8 460/7.5 Liter	G		**2%**	**2%**	**2%**	**2%**
V8 7.3L Turbo Diesel	F		**3%**	**3%**	**3%**	**2%**
SUPER CAB PICKUP—V8 (1997)						
F150 ½ Short Bed		19529	**70%**	**65%**	**60%**	**55%**
F150 ½ Long Bed		19764	**70%**	**65%**	**60%**	**55%**
4WD			**4%**	**4%**	**4%**	**4%**
Manual Trans			**(3%)**	**(3%)**	**(3%)**	**(2%)**
V6 4.2 Liter	2		**(4%)**	**(4%)**	**(3%)**	**(3%)**
V8 5.4 Liter			**1%**	**1%**	**1%**	**1%**
CREW CAB PICKUP—V8						
F250 ¾ Long Bed		23422	**62%**	**59%**	**53%**	**44%**
F350 1 Long Bed	W35H	23482	**63%**	**59%**	**53%**	**44%**
4WD	6		**4%**	**4%**	**4%**	**3%**
Manual Trans			**(2%)**	**(2%)**	**(2%)**	**(2%)**
V8 460/7.5 Liter	G		**2%**	**2%**	**2%**	**2%**
V8 7.3L Turbo Diesel	F		**3%**	**3%**	**3%**	**2%**
CAB-CHASSIS—V8						
F350 1 Cab-Ch/DR 137"	F37H	19143	**53%**	**50%**	**46%**	**38%**
F350 1 Cab-Ch/DR 161"	F37H	19297	**54%**	**51%**	**46%**	**39%**
1 Spr Dty Cb-Ch/DR 137	F47G	22518	**51%**	**48%**	**43%**	**36%**
1 Spr Dty Cb-Ch/DR 161	F47G	22673	**51%**	**48%**	**43%**	**36%**
1 Spr Dty Cb-Ch/DR 185	F47G	22833	**52%**	**49%**	**44%**	**37%**
4WD	8		**4%**	**4%**	**4%**	**3%**
V8 460/7.5 Liter	G		**2%**	**2%**	**2%**	**2%**
V8 7.3L Turbo Diesel	F		**3%**	**3%**	**3%**	**2%**

GMC TRUCKS

Body Type	VIN	List	24 Mo.	36 Mo.	48 Mo.	60 Mo.
JIMMY 4WD—V6						
Sport Utility 2D	T18W	21694	**64%**	**59%**	**54%**	**48%**
Sport Utility 4D	T13W	23742	**64%**	**59%**	**54%**	**49%**
2WD	S		**(4%)**	**(4%)**	**(4%)**	**(3%)**

NEW '96 TRUCKS/VANS

Appendix B

N.A.D.A. Official
Used Car Guide®
Examples

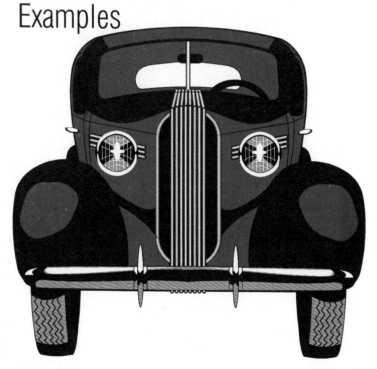

Pacific Northwest Edition

N.A.D.A.®

OFFICIAL USED CAR GUIDE-

DOMESTIC CARS—IMPORTED CARS TRUCKS

63 Years of Service

1996–APRIL–1996

Source: N.A.D.A. Official Used Car Guide®, April 1996, Pacific Northwest Edition. Used with permission of the N.A.D.A. Official Used Car Guide® Company.

Volume 63   1996–APRIL–1996   No. 4

N.A.D.A.®

OFFICIAL USED CAR GUIDE

**8400 Westpark Drive, McLean, Virginia 22102
Telephone: (703) 749-4701
(1-800) 544-6232**

Editor . . . . .Jan C. Ocean
Managing Editor .Patricia R. Erney
Domestic Vehicle Manager . . . . .William E. Winn, Jr.
Import Vehicle Manager . . . . .Cathy A. Sentnor
Commercial Vehicle Manager . . . . . . .Charles M. Wilson
Marketing Director . . . . .Lawrence S. Davis
Customer Service Manager . . . . .Michael R. Lang

N.A.D.A. OFFICIAL USED CAR GUIDE (ISSN 0027-5794) is published monthly by the N.A.D.A. Official Used Car Guide Company, 8400 Westpark Dr., McLean, Va. 22102-9985. Subscription Price is $47.00 per year. Second Class Postage paid at McLean Va. and additional mailing offices. POSTMASTER: send address changes to N.A.D.A. Official Used Car Guide Company, 8400 Westpark Dr., McLean, VA 22102-9985.

*Source: N.A.D.A. Official Used Car Guide®, April 1996, Pacific Northwest Edition.
Used with permission of the N.A.D.A. Official Used Car Guide® Company.*

IMPORTANT

EXPLANATION OF COLUMN HEADINGS

Retail   This column represents N.A.D.A.'s retail values for the region for which the Guide is designated.

**Body
Type**   The popular name for the body style.

Model   Manufacturer's Body Style number.

M.S.R.P.   This column represents N.A.D.A.'s representation of the Manufacturer's Suggested Retail Price at the time of introduction and includes manufacturer's standard equipment only. N.A.D.A.'s MSRP does not include transportation, destination or taxes.

Loan   This column represents N.A.D.A.'s projected amount of credit that may be obtained on vehicles based upon the trade-in value.

**Trade-In
or Wh'sle**   This column represents N.A.D.A.'s wholesale values for the region for which the Guide is designated.

III

Source: N.A.D.A. Official Used Car Guide®, April 1996, Pacific Northwest Edition. Used with permission of the N.A.D.A. Official Used Car Guide® Company.

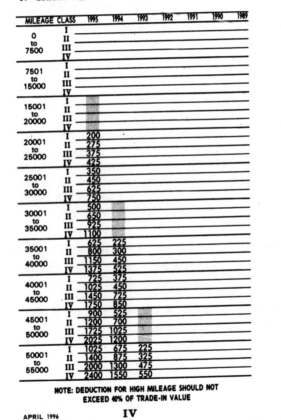

HIGH MILEAGE TABLE

VALUES SHOWN BELOW TO BE DEDUCTED FROM GUIDEBOOK VALUE

I— SUB-COMPACT AND COMPACT CARS AND COMPACT TRUCKS
II— INTERMEDIATE AND PERSONAL LUXURY CARS AND MID-SIZED TRUCKS
III— STANDARD SIZE CARS AND TRUCKS
IV— LUXURY CARS

MILEAGE CLASS		1995	1994	1993	1992	1991	1990	1989
0 to 7500	I							
	II							
	III							
	IV							
7501 to 15000	I							
	II							
	III							
	IV							
15001 to 20000	I							
	II							
	III							
	IV							
20001 to 25000	I	200						
	II	275						
	III	375						
	IV	425						
25001 to 30000	I	350						
	II	450						
	III	625						
	IV	750						
30001 to 35000	I	500						
	II	650						
	III	925						
	IV	1100						
35001 to 40000	I	625	225					
	II	800	300					
	III	1150	450					
	IV	1375	525					
40001 to 45000	I	725	375					
	II	1025	450					
	III	1450	725					
	IV	1750	850					
45001 to 50000	I	900	525					
	II	1200	700					
	III	1725	1025					
	IV	2025	1200					
50001 to 55000	I	1025	675	225				
	II	1400	875	325				
	III	2000	1300	475				
	IV	2400	1550	550				

NOTE: DEDUCTION FOR HIGH MILEAGE SHOULD NOT EXCEED 40% OF TRADE-IN VALUE

APRIL 1996   **IV**

Source: N.A.D.A. Official Used Car Guide®, April 1996, Pacific Northwest Edition.
Used with permission of the N.A.D.A. Official Used Car Guide® Company.

HIGH MILEAGE TABLE

VALUES SHOWN BELOW TO BE DEDUCTED FROM GUIDEBOOK VALUE

I— SUB-COMPACT AND COMPACT CARS AND COMPACT TRUCKS
II— INTERMEDIATE AND PERSONAL LUXURY CARS AND MID-SIZED TRUCKS
III— STANDARD SIZE CARS AND TRUCKS
IV— LUXURY CARS

MILEAGE CLASS		1995	1994	1993	1992	1991	1990	1989
55001 to 60000	I	1225	800	400				
	II	1600	1050	500				
	III	2250	1575	775				
	IV	2650	1850	900				
60001 to 65000	I	1375	925	525	225			
	II	1850	1225	700	275			
	III	2525	1850	1050	450			
	IV	2975	2175	1225	525			
65001 to 70000	I	1500	1075	675	375			
	II	2000	1400	875	475			
	III	2850	2125	1325	750			
	IV	3325	2500	1550	875			
70001 to 75000	I	1625	1200	800	525	225		
	II	2175	1625	1050	675	275		
	III	3175	2400	1575	1000	425		
	IV	3625	2775	1850	1175	525		
75001 to 80000	I	1750	1325	925	650	375		
	II	2350	1750	1225	825	475		
	III	3400	2650	1875	1300	750		
	IV	3925	3075	2175	1500	850		
80001 to 90000	I	1950	1525	1125	875	600	300	
	II	2550	2025	1500	1125	775	400	
	III	3725	3025	2275	1700	1125	575	
	IV	4375	3525	2650	1975	1325	650	
90001 to 100000	I	2175	1775	1400	1125	875	600	400
	II	2875	2375	1825	1475	1100	750	500
	III	4200	3550	2800	2225	1675	1100	750
	IV	4900	4125	3250	2600	1925	1300	850
100001 to 115000	I	2500	2075	1700	1450	1200	925	750
	II	3275	2750	2250	1875	1500	1175	950
	III	4800	4125	3400	2875	2350	1775	1475
	IV	5600	4800	4000	3350	2725	2100	1675
115001 to 130000	I	2900	2450	2075	1825	1575	1325	1175
	II	3725	3225	2750	2375	2075	1725	1500
	III	5350	4800	4125	3625	3125	2575	2275
	IV	6300	5600	4825	4225	3625	3025	2650
130001 to 150000+	I	3550	2800	2450	2250	2000	1775	1625
	II	4450	3725	3275	2975	2625	2300	2075
	III	6125	5550	4925	4450	3950	3475	2950
	IV	7150	6500	5725	5200	4625	4050	3300

NOTE: DEDUCTION FOR HIGH MILEAGE SHOULD NOT EXCEED 40% OF TRADE-IN VALUE

APRIL 1996   V

Source: N.A.D.A. Official Used Car Guide®, April 1996, Pacific Northwest Edition. Used with permission of the N.A.D.A. Official Used Car Guide® Company.

LOW MILEAGE TABLE

VALUES SHOWN BELOW TO BE ADDED TO GUIDEBOOK VALUE

I— SUB-COMPACT AND COMPACT CARS AND COMPACT TRUCKS
II— INTERMEDIATE AND PERSONAL LUXURY CARS AND MID-SIZED TRUCKS
III— STANDARD SIZE CARS AND TRUCKS
IV— LUXURY CARS

MILEAGE CLASS		1995	1994	1993	1992	1991	1990	1989
0 to 7500	I	375	775	1175	1425	1675	1925	2075
	II	425	900	1375	1675	1975	2250	2425
	III	550	1150	1750	2150	2525	2875	3100
	IV	600	1275	1950	2375	2800	3200	3450
7501 to 15000	I	200	550	975	1225	1500	1750	1900
	II	225	650	1125	1450	1750	2025	2200
	III	300	825	1450	1850	2250	2600	2825
	IV	325	925	1600	2050	2475	2900	3150
15001 to 20000	I		375	800	1075	1325	1575	1750
	II		425	925	1250	1550	1850	2025
	III		550	1200	1600	2000	2375	2600
	IV		625	1325	1775	2225	2650	2900
20001 to 25000	I		225	650	925	1200	1450	1625
	II		250	775	1100	1400	1700	1875
	III		325	975	1400	1800	2200	2425
	IV		375	1100	1550	2000	2425	2700
25001 to 30000	I		75	525	800	1075	1325	1500
	II		100	600	925	1250	1550	1725
	III		125	775	1200	1600	2000	2225
	IV		150	850	1325	1775	2225	2475
30001 to 35000	I			375	650	925	1200	1375
	II			425	775	1100	1400	1575
	III			550	975	1400	1800	2000
	IV			625	1100	1550	2000	2275
35001 to 40000	I			225	525	800	1075	1250
	II			250	600	925	1250	1425
	III			325	750	1200	1600	1850
	IV			375	825	1325	1775	2050
40001 to 45000	I			75	375	650	925	1100
	II			100	425	775	1100	1275
	III			125	550	975	1400	1650
	IV			150	600	1100	1550	1825
45001 to 50000	I				225	525	800	975
	II				250	600	925	1125
	III				325	775	1200	1450
	IV				375	850	1325	1600
50001 to 55000	I				75	375	650	825
	II				100	425	775	975
	III				125	550	975	1250
	IV				150	625	1100	1375

NOTE: ADDED PREMIUM FOR LOW MILEAGE SHOULD NOT EXCEED 50% OF TRADE-IN VALUE

APRIL 1996   VI

Source: N.A.D.A. Official Used Car Guide®, April 1996, Pacific Northwest Edition.
Used with permission of the N.A.D.A. Official Used Car Guide® Company.

LOW MILEAGE TABLE

VALUES SHOWN BELOW TO BE ADDED TO GUIDEBOOK VALUE

I— SUB-COMPACT AND COMPACT CARS AND COMPACT TRUCKS

II— INTERMEDIATE AND PERSONAL LUXURY CARS AND MID-SIZED TRUCKS

III— STANDARD SIZE CARS AND TRUCKS

IV— LUXURY CARS

MILEAGE CLASS		1995	1994	1993	1992	1991	1990	1989
55001 to 60000	I					225	525	700
	II					250	600	800
	III					325	775	1025
	IV					375	850	1150
60001 to 65000	I					75	375	550
	II					100	425	650
	III					125	550	825
	IV					150	625	925
65001 to 70000	I						225	400
	II						250	475
	III						325	600
	IV						375	675
70001 to 75000	I						75	250
	II						100	325
	III						125	400
	IV						150	450
75001 to 80000	I							100
	II							125
	III							175
	IV							200
80001 to 90000	I							
	II							
	III							
	IV							
90001 to 100000	I							
	II							
	III							
	IV							
100001 to 115000	I							
	II							
	III							
	IV							
115001 to 130000	I							
	II							
	III							
	IV							
130001 to 150000+	I							
	II							
	III							
	IV							

NOTE: ADDED PREMIUM FOR LOW MILEAGE SHOULD NOT EXCEED 50% OF TRADE-IN VALUE

APRIL 1996 — **VII**

Source: N.A.D.A. Official Used Car Guide®, April 1996, Pacific Northwest Edition. Used with permission of the N.A.D.A. Official Used Car Guide® Company.

CHEVROLET 1995-94 19

Trd-In	BODY TYPE	Model No.	M.S.R.P.	Wgt.	Loan	Retail

1994 CAVALIER·AT·PS·AC·FWD Start Sept. 1993

CAVALIER VL-L4 Veh. Ident.:()G1(Model)()()()R()000001 Up.

| 6975 | Sedan 4D | JC5 | $8995 | 2520 | 6300 | 8600 |
| 6875 | Coupe 2D | JC1 | 8845 | 2509 | 6200 | 8500 |

CAVALIER RS-L4 Veh. Ident.:()G1(Model)()()()R()000001 Up.

7675	Sedan 4D	JC5	$11315	2526	6925	9400
7575	Coupe 2D	JC1	10715	2515	6825	9275
11025	Convertible 2D	JC3	16995	2678	9925	13100

CAVALIER WAGON-L4 Veh. Ident.:()G1JC8()()()R()000001 Up.

| 8125 | Station Wagon 4D | JC8 | $11465 | 2623 | 7325 | 9925 |

CAVALIER Z24-V6 Veh. Ident.:()G1(Model)()()()R()000001 Up.

| 10675 | Coupe 2D | JF1 | $13995 | 2695 | 9625 | 12725 |
| 14125 | Convertible 2D | JF3 | 19995 | 2858 | 12725 | 16400 |

225	Add Sunroof				225	225
200	Add Compact Disc Player				200	200
150	Add Power Windows (Std. Convertible)				150	150
150	Add Cruise Control				150	150
100	Add Tilt Steering Wheel (Std. Z24)				100	100
75	Add Luggage Rack (S/W)				75	75
500	Add V6 Engine (Std. Z24)				500	500
300	Add Anti-Theft/Recovery System				300	300
400	Deduct W/out Automatic Trans.				400	400
525	Deduct W/out Air Conditioning				525	525

1994 BERETTA/CORSICA·AT·PS·AC·FWD Start Sept. 1993

BERETTA/CORSICA-L4 Veh. Ident.:()G1(Model)()()()R()000001 Up.

7775	Beretta Coupe 2D	LV1	$12415	2649	7000	9500
9300	Beretta Coupe 2D Z26 (5 Spd.)	LW1	15310	2749	8375	11225
7275	Corsica Sedan 4D	LD5	13145	2665	6550	8950

BERETTA/CORSICA-V6 Veh. Ident.:()G1(Model)()()()R()000001 Up.

8325	Beretta Coupe 2D	LV1	$13690	2749	7500	10150
10300	Beretta Coupe 2D Z26	LW1	15835	2797	9275	12325
7825	Corsica Sedan 4D	LD5	13865	2763	7050	9550

225	Add Sunroof				225	225
200	Add Compact Disc Player				200	200
150	Add Cruise Control				150	150
150	Add Power Windows				150	150
100	Add Tilt Steering Wheel				100	100
300	Add Anti-Theft/Recovery System				300	300
400	Deduct W/out Automatic Trans.				400	400

1994 LUMINA·AT·PS·AC·FWD Start Sept. 1993

LUMINA-V6 Veh. Ident.:()G1WL5()()()R()000001 Up.

| 9125 | Sedan 4D | WL5 | $15305 | 3333 | 8225 | 11125 |

LUMINA EURO-V6 Veh. Ident.:()G1(Model)()()()R()000001 Up.

| 10525 | Sedan 4D | WN5 | $16515 | 3269 | 9475 | 12625 |
| 10525 | Coupe 2D | WN1 | 16875 | 3369 | 9475 | 12625 |

LUMINA Z34-V6 Veh. Ident.:()G1WP1()()()R()000001 Up.

| 13050 | Coupe 2D | WP1 | $19310 | 3440 | 11750 | 15325 |

225	Add Compact Disc Player				225	225
225	Add Delco/Bose Music System				225	225
175	Add Cruise Control (Std. Z34)				175	175

DEDUCT FOR HIGH MILEAGE
PACIFIC NORTHWEST EDITION

c

D O M E S T I C

C A R S

Source: N.A.D.A. Official Used Car Guide®, April 1996, Pacific Northwest Edition.
Used with permission of the N.A.D.A. Official Used Car Guide® Company.

20 CHEVROLET 1994

Trd-In	BODY TYPE	Model No.	M.S.R.P.	Wgt.	Loan	Retail
1994 LUMINA-AT-PS-AC-FWD-Continued						
175	Add Power Seat				175	175
175	Add Power Windows (Std. Euro 2D, Z34)				175	175
225	Add Anti-Lock Brakes (Std. Euro, Z34)				225	225
700	Add Euro 3.4 Pkg. (Euro Sedan)				700	700
300	Add Anti-Theft/Recovery System				300	300

1994 CAMARO-AT-PS-AC   Start Sept. 1993, Conv. March 1994

CAMARO-V6   Veh. Ident.:( )G1(Model)( )( )( )R( )000001 Up.

10625	Coupe 2D	FP2	$13399	3247	9575	12725
15050	Convertible 2D	FP3	18745	3342	13550	17450

CAMARO-V8   Veh. Ident.:( )G1(Model)( )( )( )R( )000001 Up.

13700	Coupe 2D Z28	FP2	$16779	3424	12350	16025
18125	Convertible 2D Z28	FP3	22075	3524	16325	20775

750	Add T-Top	$895		750	750
225	Add Compact Disc Player			225	225
225	Add Delco/Bose Music System			225	225
125	Add Power Door Locks			125	125
175	Add Power Windows			175	175
175	Add Power Seat			175	175
175	Add Cruise Control			175	175
225	Add Custom Wheels/Covers			225	225
300	Add Anti-Theft/Recovery System			300	300
450	Deduct W/out Automatic Trans. (V6)			450	450
625	Deduct W/out Air Conditioning			625	625

1994 IMPALA-CAPRICE CLASSIC-AT-PS-AC
                 Start Sept. 1993, Impala SS March 1994

CAPRICE CLASSIC-V8   Veh. Ident.:( )G1(Model)( )( )( )R( )000001 Up.

11600	Sedan 4D	BL5	$18995	4036	10450	13900
13775	Sedan 4D LS	BN5	21435	4054	12400	16200
14200	Station Wagon 4D 3S	BL8	21180	4449	12800	16650

IMPALA-V8   Veh. Ident.:( )G1BN5( )( )( )R( )000001 Up.

18300	Sedan 4D SS	BN5	$21920	4218	16475	21075

250	Add Compact Disc Player			250	250
150	Add Power Door Locks (Std. LS, Impala)			150	150
200	Add Power Seat (Std. Impala)			200	200
200	Add Power Windows (Std. LS, Impala)			200	200
250	Add Custom Wheels/Covers			250	250
200	Add Cruise Control (Std. LS, Impala)			200	200
350	Add Leather Seats (Std. Impala)			350	350
175	Add Woodgrain (S/W)			175	175
300	Add Anti-Theft/Recovery System			300	300

1994 CORVETTE-AT/6 Spd.   Start Sept. 1993

CORVETTE-V8   Veh. Ident.:( )G1(Model)( )( )( )R( )000001 Up.

23125	Coupe 2D	YY2	$36185	3317	20825	26475
27575	Convertible 2D	YY3	42960	3358	24825	31225
40700	Coupe 2D ZR1	YZ2	67443	3503	36650	45125

325	Add Compact Disc Player (Std. ZR1)			325	325
325	Add Delco/Bose Music System (Std. ZR1)			325	325
700	Add Removable Glass Roof			700	700
950	Add Removable Hardtop	$1995		950	950
300	Add Anti-Theft/Recovery System			300	300

DEDUCT FOR RECONDITIONING
1996 APRIL 1996   c

Source: N.A.D.A. Official Used Car Guide®, April 1996, Pacific Northwest Edition. Used with permission of the N.A.D.A. Official Used Car Guide® Company.

DODGE 1994 39

Trd-In	BODY TYPE	Model No.	M.S.R.P.	Wgt.	Loan	Retail
1994 COLT-AT-PS-AC-FWD (Japan)-Continued						
225	Add Anti-Lock Brakes....................				225	225
300	Add Anti-Theft/Recovery System				300	300
350	Deduct W/out Automatic Trans.				350	350
150	Deduct W/out Power Steering				150	150
475	Deduct W/out Air Conditioning				475	475

1994 NEON-AT-PS-AC-FWD   Start Sept. 1993

NEON-4 Cyl.   Veh. Ident.:()B3()(Model)()()R()000001 Up.

Trd-In	BODY TYPE	Model No.	M.S.R.P.	Wgt.	Loan	Retail
7775	Sedan 4D S27		$9199	2311	7000	9500
8575	Sedan 4D Highline S47		11025	2379	7725	10400
9450	Sedan 4D Sport S67		13089	2440	8525	11400
150	Add Cruise Control				150	150
150	Add Power Windows....................			t	150	150
100	Add Power Door Locks (Std. Sport)				100	100
100	Add Tilt Steering Wheel (Std. Sport)				100	100
300	Add Anti-Theft/Recovery System				300	300
400	Deduct W/out Automatic Trans.				400	400
175	Deduct W/out Power Steering				175	175
525	Deduct W/out Air Conditioning				525	525

1994 SHADOW-AT-PS-AC-FWD   Start Sept. 1993

SHADOW-4 Cyl.   Veh. Ident.:1B3()(Model)()()R()000001 Up.

Trd-In	BODY TYPE	Model No.	M.S.R.P.	Wgt.	Loan	Retail
6675	Hatchback 4D P28		$9206	2643	6025	8275
6575	Hatchback 2D P24		8806	2608	5925	8175
SHADOW ES-4 Cyl. Veh. Ident.:1B3()(Model)()()R()000001 Up.						
7675	Hatchback 4D P68		$10652	2757	6925	9400
7575	Hatchback 2D P64		10252	2672	6825	9275
225	Add Sunroof..........................				225	225
200	Add Compact Disc Player................				200	200
100	Add Power Door Locks..................				100	100
150	Add Power Windows....................				150	150
150	Add Power Seat				150	150
150	Add Cruise Control				150	150
100	Add Tilt Steering Wheel.................				100	100
200	Add Custom Wheels/Covers..............				200	200
225	Add Anti-Lock Brakes..................				225	225
500	Add V6 Engine........................				500	500
300	Add Anti-Theft/Recovery System				300	300
400	Deduct W/out Automatic Trans.				400	400
525	Deduct W/out Air Conditioning				525	525

1994 SPIRIT-AT-PS-AC-FWD   Start Sept. 1993

SPIRIT-4 Cyl.   Veh. Ident.:1B3()A46()R()000001 Up.

Trd-In	BODY TYPE	Model No.	M.S.R.P.	Wgt.	Loan	Retail
7700	Sedan 4D A46		$12470	2744	6950	9525
SPIRIT-V6 Veh. Ident.:1B3()A46()()R()000001 Up.						
8300	Sedan 4D A46		$13195	2824	7475	10200
125	Add Power Door Locks..................				125	125
175	Add Power Windows....................				175	175
175	Add Power Seat				175	175
225	Add Anti-Lock Brakes..................				225	225
225	Add Custom Wheels/Covers..............				225	225
300	Add Anti-Theft/Recovery System				300	300

DEDUCT FOR HIGH MILEAGE
PACIFIC NORTHWEST EDITION

D O M E S T I C   C A R S

Source: N.A.D.A. Official Used Car Guide®, April 1996, Pacific Northwest Edition.
Used with permission of the N.A.D.A. Official Used Car Guide® Company.

40 DODGE 1994-93

Trd-In	BODY TYPE	Model No.	M.S.R.P.	Wgt.	Loan	Retail
1994 INTREPID-AT-PS-AC-FWD					**Start Sept. 1993**	
INTREPID-V6	Veh. Ident.::()B3()(Model)()()R()000001 Up.					
11525	Sedan 4D	D46	$17251	3271	10375	13825
13300	Sedan 4D ES	D56	19191	3370	11975	15700
250	Add Compact Disc Player				250	250
250	Add Infinity Stereo System				250	250
150	Add Power Door Locks				150	150
200	Add Power Windows				200	200
200	Add Power Seat				200	200
200	Add Cruise Control (Std. ES)				200	200
250	Add Custom Wheels/Covers				250	250
400	Add 3.5L V6 Engine				400	400
350	Add Leather Seats				350	350
225	Add Anti-Lock Brakes				225	225
550	Add Power Sunroof				550	550
300	Add Anti-Theft/Recovery System				300	300
1994 STEALTH-AT/5 Spd.-PS-AC-FWD					**Start Sept. 1993**	
STEALTH-V6	Veh. Ident.::JB3()(Model)()()R()000001 Up.					
15750	Liftback 2D	M44	$20935	3064	14175	18300
17450	Liftback 2D R/T	M64	23680	3164	15725	20175
23350	R/T Turbo 4WD (6 Spd.)	N74	37512	3797	21025	26500
250	Add Compact Disc Player				250	250
150	Add Power Door Locks (Std. 4WD)				150	150
325	Add Sunroof				325	325
200	Add Power Windows (Std. 4WD)				200	200
200	Add Power Seat (Std. 4WD)				200	200
200	Add Cruise Control (Std. 4WD)				200	200
250	Add Custom Wheels/Covers				250	250
350	Add Leather Seats				350	350
225	Add Anti-Lock Brakes (Std. 4WD)				225	225
300	Add Anti-Theft/Recovery System				300	300
675	Deduct W/out Air Conditioning				675	675
1993 COLT-AT-PS-AC-FWD (Japan)					**Start Oct. 1992**	
COLT-4 Cyl.	Veh. Ident.::JB3()(Model)()()P()000001 Up.					
4650	Sedan 2D (5 Spd.)	A11	$7806	2085	4200	6050
5925	Sedan 4D	A26	9448	2195	5350	7475
5375	Sedan 2D GL	A21	8705	2105	4850	6875
6300	Sedan 4D GL	A46	10423	2290	5675	7875
75	Add Power Door Locks				75	75
125	Add Power Windows				125	125
75	Add Tilt Steering Wheel				75	75
125	Add Cruise Control				125	125
175	Add Custom Wheels/Covers				175	175
200	Add Anti-Lock Brakes				200	200
250	Add Anti-Theft/Recovery System				250	250
300	Deduct W/out Automatic Trans.				300	300
125	Deduct W/out Power Steering				125	125
425	Deduct W/out Air Conditioning				425	425
1993 SHADOW-AT-PS-AC-FWD					**Start Oct. 1992**	
SHADOW-4 Cyl.	Veh. Ident.::1B3()(Model)()()P()000001 Up.					
5875	Hatchback 4D	P28	$8797	2610	5300	7425
5775	Hatchback 2D	P24	8397	2575	5200	7300

DEDUCT FOR RECONDITIONING
1996 APRIL 1996

c

58 FORD 1995-94

Trd-In	BODY TYPE	Model No.	M.S.R.P.	Wgt.	Loan	Retail

D O M E S T I C   C A R S

1994 ASPIRE·AC·FWD (Korea)

Start Feb. 1994

ASPIRE-4 Cyl. Veh. Ident..()FA()T(Model)()()R()100001 Up.

5325	Hatchback 2D	05	$8240	2004	**4800**	**6825**
5625	Hatchback 4D	06	8855	2053	**5075**	**7150**
5875	Hatchback 2D SE	07	8995	.2004	**5300**	**7425**

200	Add Compact Disc Player	**200**	**200**
200	Add Custom Wheels/Covers	**200**	**200**
225	Add Anti-Lock Brakes	**225**	**225**
300	Add Anti-Theft/Recovery System	**300**	**300**
350	Add Automatic Trans.	**350**	**350**
150	Add Power Steering	**150**	**150**
475	Deduct W/out Air Conditioning	**475**	**475**

1994 ESCORT·AT·PS·AC·FWD

Start Dec. 1993

ESCORT-4 Cyl. Veh. Ident.:()FA()P(Model)()()R()100001 Up.

6125	Hatchback 2D	10	$9035	2304	**5525**	**7675**
6800	Hatchback 2D LX	11	9890	2325	**6125**	**8400**
7100	Hatchback 4D LX	14	10325	2419	**6400**	**8775**
7200	Sedan 4D LX	13	10550	2371	**6500**	**8875**
7650	Station Wagon 4D LX	15	10880	2419	**6900**	**9375**
8150	Hatchback 2D GT	12	12300	2447	**7350**	**9950**

100	Add Power Door Locks	**100**	**100**
150	Add Cruise Control	**150**	**150**
350	Add Power Sunroof	**350**	**350**
200	Add Compact Disc Player	**200**	**200**
150	Add Power Windows	**150**	**150**
100	Add Tilt Steering Wheel	**100**	**100**
75	Add Luggage Rack (S/W)	**75**	**75**

DEDUCT FOR RECONDITIONING
1996 APRIL 1996

c

Source: N.A.D.A. Official Used Car Guide®, April 1996, Pacific Northwest Edition.
Used with permission of the N.A.D.A. Official Used Car Guide® Company.

FORD 1994 59

Trd-In	BODY TYPE	Model No.	M.S.R.P.	Wgt.	Loan	Retail
1994 ESCORT-AT-PS-AC-FWD-Continued						
200	Add Custom Wheels/Covers				200	200
225	Add Anti-Lock Brakes				225	225
300	Add Anti-Theft/Recovery System				300	300
350	Deduct W/out Automatic Trans.				350	350
150	Deduct W/out Power Steering				150	150
475	Deduct W/out Air Conditioning				475	475
1994 TEMPO-AT-PS-AC-FWD					**Start Sept. 1993**	
TEMPO GL-4 Cyl.	Veh. Ident.:()FA()P(Model)()()R()100001 Up.					
6800	Sedan 2D	31	$10735	2511	6125	8550
6900	Sedan 4D	36	10735	2569	6225	8675
TEMPO LX-4 Cyl.	Veh. Ident.:()FA()P37()()R()100001 Up.					
7800	Sedan 4D	37	$12560	2569	7025	9625
150	Add Power Windows				150	150
100	Add Power Door Locks (Std. LX)				100	100
150	Add Power Seat				150	150
150	Add Cruise Control				150	150
100	Add Tilt Steering Wheel (Std. LX)				100	100
200	Add Custom Wheels/Covers				200	200
200	Add Driver Side Air Bag				200	200
500	Add V6 Engine				500	500
300	Add Anti-Theft/Recovery System				300	300
400	Deduct W/out Automatic Trans.				400	400
525	Deduct W/out Air Conditioning				525	525
1994 MUSTANG-AT-PS-AC			**Start Dec. 1993, Cobra March 1994**			
MUSTANG-V6	Veh. Ident.:()FA()P(Model)()()R()100001 Up.					
10950	Coupe 2D	40	$13355	3055	9875	13075
14700	Convertible 2D	44	20150	3193	13250	17075
MUSTANG-V8	Veh. Ident.:()FA()P(Model)()()R()100001 Up.					
13550	Coupe 2D GT	42	$17270	3258	12200	15875
17300	Convertible 2D GT	45	21960	3414	15575	19900
17050	Hatchback 2D Cobra (5 Spd.)	42	20765		15350	19625
20800	Convertible 2D Cobra (5 Spd.)	45	23535		18725	23600
225	Add Compact Disc Player				225	225
125	Add Power Door Locks (Base Coupe)				125	125
175	Add Power Windows (Base Coupe)				175	175
175	Add Cruise Control (Std. Cobra)				175	175
225	Add Custom Wheels/Covers				225	225
300	Add Leather Seats				300	300
225	Add Anti-Lock Brakes (Std. Cobra)				225	225
300	Add Anti-Theft/Recovery System				300	300
400	Deduct W/out Automatic Trans. (V6)				400	400
625	Deduct W/out Air Conditioning				625	625
1994 PROBE-AT-PS-AC-FWD					**Start Oct. 1993**	
PROBE-4 Cyl.	Veh. Ident.:1ZV()P(Model)()()R()100001 Up.					
9100	Hatchback 2D	20	$13685	2690	8200	11100
11100	Hatchback 2D GT (V6)	22	16015	2921	10000	13225
225	Add Compact Disc Player				225	225
125	Add Power Door Locks				125	125
175	Add Power Windows				175	175
175	Add Power Seat				175	175
500	Add Power Sunroof				500	500

DEDUCT FOR HIGH MILEAGE
PACIFIC NORTHWEST EDITION

c

D O M E S T I C   C A R S

60 **FORD 1994**

Trd-In	BODY TYPE	Model No.	M.S.R.P.	Wgt.	Loan	Retail
1994 PROBE-AT-PS-AC-FWD-Continued						
300	Add Leather Seats				300	300
175	Add Cruise Control				175	175
125	Add Tilt Steering Wheel				125	125
225	Add Custom Wheels/Covers				225	225
225	Add Anti-Lock Brakes				225	225
300	Add Anti-Theft/Recovery System				300	300
400	Deduct W/out Automatic Trans.				400	400
625	Deduct W/out Air Conditioning				625	625

1994 TAURUS-AT-PS-AC-FWD — Start Sept. 1993

TAURUS-V6 Veh. Ident.:()FA()P(Model)()()R()100001 Up.

Trd-In	BODY TYPE	Model No.	M.S.R.P.	Wgt.	Loan	Retail
9975	Sedan 4D GL	52	$16140	3104	9000	12025
11175	Station Wagon 4D GL	57	17220	3253	10075	13300
11475	Sedan 4D LX	53	18785	3147	10350	13625
12675	Station Wagon 4D LX	58	20400	3296	11425	14950

TAURUS SHO-V6 Veh. Ident.:()FA()P54()()R()100001 Up.

Trd-In	BODY TYPE	Model No.	M.S.R.P.	Wgt.	Loan	Retail
14125	Sedan 4D	54	$24715	3395	12725	16475
225	Add Compact Disc Player				225	225
225	Add JBL Stereo System				225	225
500	Add Power Sunroof				500	500
125	Add Power Door Locks (Std. LX, SHO)				125	125
175	Add Power Windows (Std. LX, SHO)				175	175
175	Add Power Seat (Std. LX, SHO)				175	175
175	Add Cruise Control (Std. SHO)				175	175
225	Add Custom Wheels/Covers				225	225
300	Add Leather Seats				300	300
175	Add Third Seat S/W				175	175
350	Add 3.8L V6 Engine (Std. LX S/W)				350	350
225	Add Anti-Lock Brakes (Std. SHO)				225	225
300	Add Anti-Theft/Recovery System				300	300
450	Deduct W/out Automatic Trans.				450	450
625	Deduct W/out Air Conditioning				625	625

1994 CROWN VICTORIA-AT-PS-AC — Start Sept. 1993

CROWN VICTORIA-V8 Veh. Ident.:()FA()P(Model)()()R()100001 Up.

Trd-In	BODY TYPE	Model No.	M.S.R.P.	Wgt.	Loan	Retail
11150	Sedan 4D S	72	$20000	3786	10050	13425
12125	Sedan 4D	73	19300	3786	10925	14450
13025	Sedan 4D LX	74	20715	3794	11725	15400
250	Add Compact Disc Player				250	250
250	Add JBL Stereo System				250	250
150	Add Power Door Locks				150	150
200	Add Power Seat (Std. LX)				200	200
200	Add Cruise Control				200	200
250	Add Custom Wheels/Covers				250	250
350	Add Leather Seats				350	350
225	Add Anti-Lock Brakes				225	225
300	Add Anti-Theft/Recovery System				300	300

1994 THUNDERBIRD-AT-PS-AC — Start Oct. 1993

THUNDERBIRD-V6 Veh. Ident.:()FA()P(Model)()()R()100001 Up.

Trd-In	BODY TYPE	Model No.	M.S.R.P.	Wgt.	Loan	Retail
10700	Coupe 2D LX	62	$16830	3570	9650	12800
14575	Super Coupe 2D	64	22240	3758	13125	16950

THUNDERBIRD-V8 Veh. Ident.:()FA()P62()()R()100001 Up.

Trd-In	BODY TYPE	Model No.	M.S.R.P.	Wgt.	Loan	Retail
11300	Coupe 2D LX	62	$17860	3711	10175	13425

DEDUCT FOR RECONDITIONING
1996 APRIL 1996

c

D O M E S T I C   C A R S

Source: N.A.D.A. Official Used Car Guide®, April 1996, Pacific Northwest Edition. Used with permission of the N.A.D.A. Official Used Car Guide® Company.

PONTIAC 1995-94 105

Trd-In	BODY TYPE	Model No.	M.S.R.P.	Wgt.	Loan	Retail

1994 SUNBIRD-AT-PS-AC-FWD Start Sept. 1993

SUNBIRD LE-L4   Veh. Ident.:( )G2(Model)( )( )( )R( )000001 Up.

7425	Sedan 4D	JB5	$9764	2502	6700	9125
7325	Coupe 2D	JB1	9764	2484	6600	9025
10775	Convertible 2D	JB3	15524	2661	9700	12825

SUNBIRD SE-V6   Veh. Ident.:( )G2JL1( )( )( )R( )000001 Up.

9725	Coupe 2D	JL1	$12424	2682	8775	11700

225	Add Sunroof	225	225
200	Add Compact Disc Player	200	200
150	Add Power Windows (Std. Convertible)	150	150
100	Add Tilt Steering Wheel	100	100
200	Add Custom Wheels/Covers	200	200
150	Add Cruise Control	150	150
500	Add V6 Engine (Std. SE)	500	500
300	Add Anti-Theft/Recovery System	300	300
400	Deduct W/out Automatic Trans.	400	400
525	Deduct W/out Air Conditioning	525	525

1994 GRAND AM-AT-PS-AC-FWD Start Sept. 1993

GRAND AM SE-Quad 4   Veh. Ident.:( )G2(Model)( )( )( )R( )000001 Up.

9175	Sedan 4D	NE5	$12614	2793	8275	11175
9375	Coupe 2D	NE1	12514	2736	8450	11375

GRAND AM SE-V6   Veh. Ident.:( )G2(Model)( )( )( )R( )000001 Up.

9375	Sedan 4D	NE5	$13024	2811	8450	11375
9575	Coupe 2D	NE1	12924	2754	8625	11600

GRAND AM GT-Quad 4   Veh. Ident.:( )G2(Model)( )( )( )R( )000001 Up.

11075	Sedan 4D	NW5	$15114	2882	9975	13200
11275	Coupe 2D	NW1	15014	2822	10150	13400

GRAND AM GT-V6   Veh. Ident.:( )G2(Model)( )( )( )R( )000001 Up.

11175	Sedan 4D	NW5	$14974	2915	10075	13300
11375	Coupe 2D	NW1	14874	2855	10250	13525

C   **DEDUCT FOR HIGH MILEAGE**
PACIFIC NORTHWEST EDITION

Source: N.A.D.A. Official Used Car Guide®, April 1996, Pacific Northwest Edition. Used with permission of the N.A.D.A. Official Used Car Guide® Company.

DOMESTIC CARS

106 **PONTIAC 1994**

Trd-In	BODY TYPE	Model No.	M.S.R.P.	Wgt.	Loan	Retail
1994 GRAND AM-AT-PS-AC-FWD-Continued						
225	Add Compact Disc Player				225	225
175	Add Power Windows				175	175
175	Add Power Seat				175	175
125	Add Tilt Steering Wheel (Std. GT)				125	125
225	Add Custom Wheels/Covers				225	225
175	Add Cruise Control				175	175
300	Add Leather Seats				300	300
300	Add Anti-Theft/Recovery System				300	300
450	Deduct W/out Automatic Trans.				450	450
625	Deduct W/out Air Conditioning				625	625
1994 FIREBIRD-AT-PS-AC		**Start Sept. 1993, Conv. March 1994**				
FIREBIRD-V6	Veh. Ident.:()G2(Model)()()()R()000001 Up.					
11250	Coupe 2D	FS2	$13995	3232	10125	13375
16150	Convertible 2D	FV3	21179	3346	14550	18600
FIREBIRD-V8	Veh. Ident.:()G2(Model)()()()R()000001 Up.					
14425	Coupe 2D Formula	FV2	$17995	3369	13000	16775
19325	Convertible 2D Formula	FV3	24279	3485	17400	22025
15625	Coupe 2D Trans Am	FV2	19895	3461	14075	18050
16375	Coupe 2D Trans Am GT	FV2	21395	3478	14750	18850
21275	Convertible 2D Trans Am GT	FV3	26479		19150	24100
750	Add T-Top				750	750
225	Add Compact Disc Player				225	225
125	Add Power Door Locks (Std. Trans Am, Conv.)				125	125
175	Add Power Windows (Std. Trans Am, Conv.)				175	175
175	Add Cruise Control (Std. Trans Am, Conv.)				175	175
300	Add Leather Seats				300	300
175	Add Power Seat				175	175
300	Add Anti-Theft/Recovery System				300	300
450	Deduct W/out Automatic Trans. (V6)				450	450
625	Deduct W/out Air Conditioning				625	625
1994 BONNEVILLE-AT-PS-AC-FWD				**Start Sept. 1993**		
BONNEVILLE-V6	Veh. Ident.:()G2(Model)()()()R()000001 Up.					
12450	Sedan 4D SE	HX5	$20424	3446	11225	14800
16950	Sedan 4D SSE	HZ5	25884	3587	15275	19575
550	Add Power Sunroof				550	550
250	Add Compact Disc Player				250	250
200	Add Power Seat (Std. SSE)				200	200
200	Add Cruise Control (Std. SSE)				200	200
250	Add Custom Wheels/Covers				250	250
350	Add Leather Seats				350	350
900	Add SSEi Pkg.				900	900
300	Add Anti-Theft/Recovery System				300	300
1994 GRAND PRIX-AT-PS-AC-FWD				**Start Sept. 1993**		
GRAND PRIX SE-V6	Veh. Ident.:()G2(Model)()()()R()000001 Up.					
11025	Sedan 4D	WJ5	$16174	3370	9925	13150
11025	Coupe 2D	WJ1	16770	3275	9925	13150
500	Add Power Sunroof				500	500
225	Add Compact Disc Player				225	225
175	Add Power Seat				175	175
175	Add Cruise Control (Std. Coupe)				175	175
225	Add Custom Wheels/Covers				225	225

DEDUCT FOR RECONDITIONING
1996 APRIL 1996

C

Source: N.A.D.A. Official Used Car Guide®, April 1996, Pacific Northwest Edition. Used with permission of the N.A.D.A. Official Used Car Guide® Company.

PONTIAC 1994-93 107

Trd-In	BODY TYPE	Model No.	M.S.R.P.	Wgt.	Loan	Retail
1994 GRAND PRIX-AT-PS-AC-FWD-Continued						
550	Add 3.4L V6 Engine (Std. GT, GTP)				550	550
825	Add GT Performance Pkg.				825	825
850	Add GTP Performance Pkg.				850	850
300	Add Leather Seats				300	300
225	Add Anti-Lock Brakes				225	225
300	Add Anti-Theft/Recovery System				300	300

D O M E S T I C   C A R S

JAGUAR (British) 1995-91 I-25

Trd-In	BODY TYPE	Model No.	M.S.R.P.	Wgt.	Loan	Retail

MILEAGE CATEGORY: Jaguar-IV

1995 JAGUAR-AT-PS-AC Start Sept. 1994; XJS July 1994
Veh. Ident.: SAJ(Model)()()()SC000001 Up.

Trd-In	BODY TYPE	Model No.	M.S.R.P.	Wgt.	Loan	Retail
39700	Sedan 4D XJ6	HX1	$53450	4080	35750	44050
44150	Sedan 4D XJ6 Vanden Plas	KX1	62200	4105	39750	48750
46275	Sedan 4D XJR	PX1	65000	4215	41650	51000
53000	Sedan 4D XJ12	MX1	77250	4420	47700	58100
36600	Coupe 2D XJS6	NX5	53400	3805	32950	40775
46575	Coupe 2D XJS12	NX5	72350	4053	41925	51300
40950	Convertible 2D XJS6	NX2	61550	3980	36875	45375
50925	Convertible 2D XJS12	NX2	82550	4306	45850	55900
375	Add Compact Disc Player (XJ6, XJS6)				375	375
650	Add Power Sunroof (Base XJ6)				650	650
1150	Add Traction Control (XJ6, XJS6)				1150	1150
350	Add Anti-Theft/Recovery System				350	350
600	Deduct W/out Automatic Trans.				600	600

1994 JAGUAR-AT-PS-AC
Start June 1993; XJ12 April 1993; XJ6 Sept. 1993
Veh. Ident.: SAJ(Model)()()()RC000001 Up.

Trd-In	BODY TYPE	Model No.	M.S.R.P.	Wgt.	Loan	Retail
31300	Sedan 4D XJ6	HX1	$51750	4075	28175	35175
34925	Sedan 4D XJ6 Vanden Plas	KX1	59400	4105	31450	39025
43125	Sedan 4D XJ12	MX1	71750	4401	38825	47675
31050	Coupe 2D XJS6	NX5	51950	3805	27950	34900
40125	Coupe 2D XJS12	NX5	69950	4053	36125	44500
35825	Convertible 2D XJS6	NX2	59950	4022	32075	39750
44700	Convertible 2D XJS12	NX2	79950	4306	40250	49325
325	Add Compact Disc Player (Std. XJ12)				325	325
600	Add Power Sunroof (Base XJ6)				600	600
300	Add Anti-Theft/Recovery System				300	300
550	Deduct W/out Automatic Trans.				550	550

1993 JAGUAR-AT-PS-AC Start Sept. 1992
Veh. Ident.: SAJ(Model)()()()PC000001 Up.

Trd-In	BODY TYPE	Model No.	M.S.R.P.	Wgt.	Loan	Retail
25625	Sedan 4D XJ6	HW1	$49750	4024	23075	29150
28500	Sedan 4D XJ6 Vanden Plas	KW1	56750	4035	25650	32200
26375	Coupe 2D XJS	NW5	49750	3725	23750	29950
31300	Convertible 2D XJS	NW4	56750	3950	28175	35175
300	Add Compact Disc Player				300	300
550	Add Power Sunroof (Base XJ6)				550	550
250	Add Anti-Theft/Recovery System				250	250
500	Deduct W/out Automatic Trans.				500	500

1992 JAGUAR-AT-PS-AC Start Sept. 1991
Veh. Ident.: SAJ(Model)()4()NC000001 Up.

Trd-In	BODY TYPE	Model No.	M.S.R.P.	Wgt.	Loan	Retail
18075	Sedan 4D XJ6	FY1	$44500	3935	16275	21050
20125	Sedan 4D XJ6 Sovereign	HY1	49500	3979	18125	23225
22425	Sedan 4D XJ6 Vanden Plas	KY1	54500	4035	20200	25725
23875	Sedan 4D XJ6 Majestic	MY1	59500	4035	21500	27275
23425	Coupe 2D XJS	NW5	60500	4050	21100	26800
28750	Convertible 2D XJS	NW4	67500	4250	25875	32475

I M P O R T S

*Source: N.A.D.A. Official Used Car Guide®, April 1996, Pacific Northwest Edition.
Used with permission of the N.A.D.A. Official Used Car Guide® Company.*

LEXUS (Japanese) 1995-92 I-27

Trd-In	BODY TYPE	Model No.	M.S.R.P.	Wgt.	Loan	Retail

1994 LEXUS-AT-PS-AC   **Start Sept. 1993**

Veh. Ident.: JT8 ( ) (Model) ( ) ( ) R0000001 Up.

22950	Sedan 4D ES300 .... K13		$30600	3374	20675	26300
28375	Coupe 2D SC300 .... Z31		38000	3515	25550	32075
28350	Sedan 4D GS300 .... S47		39900	3660	25525	32050
32850	Coupe 2D SC400 .... Z30		45100	3616	29575	36825
34050	Sedan 4D LS400 .... F11		49900	3859	30650	38100
600	Add Power Sunroof...				600	600
400	Add Nakamichi Stereo..				400	400
325	Add Compact Disc Player.......................................				325	325
650	Add Leather Seats (Std. SC400, LS400)..........				650	650
1000	Add Traction Control				1000	1000
300	Add Anti-Theft/Recovery System				300	300
550	Deduct W/out Automatic Trans.				550	550

1993 LEXUS-AT-PS-AC   **Start Sept. 1992**

Veh. Ident.: JT8 ( ) (Model) ( ) ( ) P0000001 Up.

19950	Sedan 4D ES300 .... K13		$27500	3362	17975	23050
25925	Coupe 2D SC300 .... Z31		34700	3495	23350	29450
25250	Sedan 4D GS300 .... S47		37500	3625	22725	28750
29700	Coupe 2D SC400 .... Z30		41400	3585	26750	33475
29125	Sedan 4D LS400 .... F11		46600	3858	26225	32875
550	Add Power Sunroof...				550	550
350	Add Nakamichi Stereo..				350	350
300	Add Compact Disc Player.......................................				300	300
575	Add Leather Seats (Std. SC400, LS400)..........				575	575
850	Add Traction Control				850	850
250	Add Anti-Theft/Recovery System				250	250
500	Deduct W/out Automatic Trans				500	500

IMPORTS

Source: N.A.D.A. Official Used Car Guide®, April 1996, Pacific Northwest Edition. Used with permission of the N.A.D.A. Official Used Car Guide® Company.

TRUCK OPTIONS

T-2

VALUES SHOWN BELOW TO BE ADDED OR DEDUCTED FROM TRUCK'S GUIDEBOOK VALUE
TRIM LEVEL VALUES DO NOT INCLUDE THE FOLLOWING EQUIPMENT

	1995	1994	1993	1992	1991	1990	1989
Rear Air Conditioning	650	575	525	425	375	325	275
Power Door Locks	150	125	100	75	50		
Power Windows	200	175	150	125	100		
Power Seat	200	175	150	125	100		
Cruise Control	200	175	150	125	100		
Tilt Wheel	150	125	100	75	50		
Luggage Rack	150	125	100	75	50		
Captain Chairs-2	250	225	200	175	150	125	
Captain Chairs-4	450	425	400	350	300	250	
Leather Seats	400	350	325	275	225		
Compact Disc Player	300	250	225	175	150		
Premium Sound System	300	250	225	175	150		
Sliding Rear Window	125	100	75	50	25		
Sunroof	350	325	300	250	200		
Dual Sunroof	850	800	750	650	550		
Power Sunroof	600	550	500	450	400		
Sunscreen Glass	250	225	175	150	125	100	
Auxiliary Fuel Tank	150	125	100	75	50		
Custom Wheels	250	225	200	175	150		
Dual Rear Wheels	950	825	700	600	525	450	400
Roll Bar	225	200	175	150	125	100	
Bed Liner	225	200	175	150	125	100	
Anti-Theft/Recovery System	350	300	250				
Running Boards	250	225	175	150	125	100	
Fiberglass Cap (Pickups)	450	400	350	300	250	200	125
Trailer Towing/Camper Package	325	300	250	200	150	125	
Stake Body	800	750	700	650	550	500	400
Extended WB Van	200	175	150	125	100	75	50
7/8 Passenger Package	275	250	225	200	175	150	100
11/12 Passenger Package	500	450	400	350	300	250	200
15 Passenger Package	650	600	550	475	425	375	325
4 Wheel Drive-Compact/Midsize	2550	2400	2250	2050	1950	1750	1700
4 Wheel Drive-Fullsize	2200	2050	1950	1800	1700	1600	1500
Winch	425	400	375	350	325	275	225
Snow Plow Package/Plow	1750	1650	1550	1450	1325	1200	1100
V8 460 Engine (Ford)	900	850	800	750	700	650	550
V8 454 Engine (GM)	900	850	800	750	700	650	550
Deduct 3/4 Speed Transmission	750	700	650	600	475	425	
Deduct 5 Speed Transmission	650	600	550	500	425	375	
Deduct W/out Power Steering	200	175	150	125	100	75	
Deduct W/out Air Conditioning	750	700	650	600	525	475	
Medium Duty							
Air Conditioning	1200	1100	1000	900	800	725	650
Aluminum Body			900	800	750	700	650
6 Speed Transmission	700	650	600	550	500	400	350
9/10 Speed Transmission	1600	1500	1400	1300	1200	1100	950
2 Speed Rear Axle	875	800	725	650	600	500	400
Air Brakes	1500	1400	1300	1150	1050	950	900
Tandem Drive Rear Axle	2850	2700	2550	2400	2100	1700	1300
Automatic Transmission	1200	1100	1000	900	850	775	700
Deduct 6 Cyl. Engine-Step Vans			600	550	500	400	350
Deduct Manual Trans.-Step Vans			600	550	500	450	400

1996 APRIL 1996

*Source: N.A.D.A. Official Used Car Guide®, April 1996, Pacific Northwest Edition.
Used with permission of the N.A.D.A. Official Used Car Guide® Company.*

T-20 **CHEVROLET 1994**

Trd-In	BODY TYPE	Model No.	M.S.R.P.	Wgt.	Loan	Retail
1994 CHEVROLET·AT·PS·AC						

K1500 BLAZER: ½ Ton. 4WD GVW 6250-6450. **W.B.** 111.5. V8 350 CID (5.7L). Tires LT225/75R16C.

18550	Utility	K18	$21125	4757	16700	21425
1000	Add Sport Trim				1000	1000
900	Add Silverado Trim				900	900
1150	Add V8 6.5L Turbo Diesel Engine				1150	1150

S10 BLAZER: ½ Ton. GVW 4350-5100. **W.B.** 100.5-107. V6 262 CID (4.3L). Tires P205/75R15.

13100	Tailgate 2D	S18	$15938	3205	11800	15550
14750	Tailgate 4D	S13	16728	3446	13275	17325
14800	Tailgate 2D 4WD	T18	17239	3506	13325	17375
16450	Tailgate 4D 4WD	T13	18962	3811	14825	19125
750	Add Tahoe Trim (Std. 4 Door)				750	750
1500	Add Tahoe LT Trim				1500	1500

ASTRO: ½ Ton. GVW 5400-6100. **W.B.** 111. V6 262 CID (4.3L). Tires P205/75R15, Ext. P215/75R15.

9800	Cargo Van	M15	$15344	3653	8825	12025
10875	Extended Cargo Van	M19	15817	3741	9800	13175
11500	Van CS	M15	16278	3998	10350	13875
12575	Extended Van CS	M19	16580	4064	11325	15000
800	Add CL Trim				800	800
1300	Add LT Trim				1300	1300
1400	Add All Wheel Drive				1400	1400

LUMINA: FWD GVW 5126. **W.B.** 109.8. V6 191 CID (3.1L). Tires P205/75R15.

9825	Cargo Van	U05	$15485	3344	8850	12050
11925	Wagon	U06	16815	3554	10750	14325
700	Add LS Trim				700	700
300	Add Power Sliding Door				300	300
475	Add 3.8L V6 Engine				475	475

G10: ½ Ton. GVW 6000. **W.B.** 110-125. V8 305 CID (5.0L). Tires P215/75R15.

13125	Chevy Van 110"	G15	$15709	3876	11825	15575

G20: ¾ Ton. GVW 6600-6875. **W.B.** 110-125. V8 350 CID (5.7L). Tires P225/75R15.

13425	Chevy Van 110"	G25	$15678	3905	12100	15900
14950	Sportvan 125"	G25	18648	4625	13475	17525

G30: 1 Ton. GVW 7100-10,500. **W.B** 125-146. V8 350 CID (5.7L). Tires LT225/75R16.

13950	Chevy Van 125"	G35	$16010	4380	12575	17300
15300	Sportvan 125"	G35	20000	5266	13775	18750
14700	Extended Chevy Van 146"	G39	18130	4881	13250	18100
16050	Extended Sportvan 146"	G39	21156	5642	14450	19550
13100	Cutaway 125"	G31	16738	4032	11800	16375
1150	Add Beauville Trim				1150	1150
750	Add V8 6.5L Diesel Engine				750	750
650	Deduct V6 Engine				650	650

T
R **SUBURBAN C1500/C2500: ½-¾ Ton. GVW** 6800-8600. **W.B.** 131.5. V8 350 CID (5.7L). Tires
U P235/75R15, C26 LT245/75R16.

C 20825	Suburban C1500	C16	$20166	4672	18750	23850
21725	Suburban C2500	C26	21398	5227	19575	24800
K 900	Add Silverado Trim				900	900
1150	Add V8 6.5L Turbo Diesel Engine				1150	1150

S
S10: ½ Ton. GVW 4200-5150. **W.B.** 108.3-122.9. V6 262 CID (4.3L). Tires P205/75R15.

8650	Pickup Fleetside 6'	S14	$9655	2905	7800	10775
8750	Pickup Fleetside 7½'	S14	9955	3000	7875	10900
11000	Pickup Fleetside Ext. Cab 6'	S19	11790	3157	9900	13325
600	Add LS Trim (Std. S19)				600	600
650	Add SS Trim				650	650
600	Deduct 4 Cyl. Engine				600	600

SEE PAGE T-2 FOR ADDITIONAL OPTIONS
1996 APRIL 1996

c

CHEVROLET 1994-93 T-21

Trd-In	BODY TYPE	Model No.	M.S.R.P.	Wgt.	Loan	Retail
1994 CHEVROLET-AT-PS-AC-Continued						
C1500: ½ Ton. GVW 5600-6800. **W.B.** 117.5-155.5. V8 305 CID (5.0L). Tires P225/75R15, Ext. Cab P235/75R15.						
10300	Pickup Fleetside "WT" 6½' (V6)	C14	$12354	3675	9275	12550
10400	Pickup Fleetside "WT" 8' (V6)	C14	12554	3815	9375	12675
13350	Pickup Sportside 6½'	C14	14690	3748	12025	15825
12950	Pickup Fleetside 6½'	C14	14027	3725	11675	15400
13050	Pickup Fleetside 8'	C14	14307	3865	11750	15500
15000	Pickup Fleetside Ext. Cab 6½'	C19	15854	4110	13500	17575
15100	Pickup Fleetside Ext. Cab 8'	C19	16697	4247	13600	17700
15400	Pickup Sportside Ext. Cab 6½'	C19	16266	4133	13875	18000
C2500: ¾ Ton. GVW 7200-8600. **W.B.** 131.5-155.5. V8 350 CID (5.7L). Tires LT225/75R16.						
13250	Ch & Cab	C24	$16233	4007	11925	15725
13800	Pickup Fleetside 8'	C24	15114	4006	12425	16300
15750	Pickup Fleetside Ext. Cab 6½'	C29	17642	4270	14175	18375
15850	Pickup Fleetside Ext. Cab 8'	C29	18529	4337	14275	18500
C3500: 1 Ton. GVW 9000-15,000. **W.B.** 131.5-183.5. V8 350 CID (5.7L), HD V8 454 CID (7.4L). Tires LT245/75R16, C39, HD Dual Rear Wheels P225/70R19.5.						
13950	Ch & Cab	C34	$17029	4273	12575	17300
14500	Pickup Fleetside 8'	C34	16847	4649	13050	17875
17375	Pickup Fleetside Ext. Cab 8'	C39	20092	5325	15650	21025
17125	Pickup Fleetside Crew Cab 8'	C33	19356	5290	15425	20775
16575	Ch & Crew Cab	C33	18579	4915	14925	20125
16750	Ch & Cab Heavy Duty	C34	20025	5281	15075	20300
800	Add Sport Trim				800	800
750	Add Silverado Trim				750	750
750	Add V8 6.5L Diesel Engine				750	750
1150	Add V8 6.5L Turbo Diesel Engine (Std. HD)				1150	1150
650	Deduct V6 Engine				650	650
MEDIUM-DUTY TRUCKS-5 Spd.-PS						
KODIAK SERIES						
C6H042 (C60): GVW 20,660-25,740. **W.B.** 132-261. (6.6L) Diesel. Tires 235/80R22.5G, LoPro 225/70R19.5F.						
19650	Ch & Cab	6H1	$28400	6762	17700	23475
20100	Ch & Cab LoPro	6H1	27200	6523	18100	23950
C7H042 (C70): GVW 22,440-36,220. **W.B.** 144-261. (6.6L) Diesel. Tires 235/80R22.5G.						
20600	Ch & Cab	7H1	$29350	7058	18550	24500
3000	Deduct Gas Engine				3000	3000
MEDIUM DUTY CABOVER-5 Spd.-PS						
W4S042: GVW 11,050-14,250. **W.B.** 109-150. V8 350 CID (5.7L), 4 Cyl. 236 CID (3.9L) T-Diesel. Tires 215/85R16E.						
13700	Ch & Tilt Cab T-Diesel	4B1K	$22832	5019	12350	17025
11700	Ch & Tilt Cab Gas (AT)	4B1A	19932	4850	10550	14800
W5R042: GVW 18,000. **W.B.** 113-177. 6 Cyl. 396 CID (6.5L) T-Diesel. Tires 215/75R17.5F.						
15600	Ch & Tilt Cab	5B1	$30800	6480	14050	19075
W6R042: GVW 20,500-22,000. **W.B.** 144-213. 6 Cyl. 396 CID (6.5L) T-Diesel. Tires 9R22.5F.						
17800	Ch & Tilt Cab	6A1	$35484	7960	16025	21500
19350	Ch & Tilt Cab LoPro (AT)	6A1	38120	7905	17425	23150
W7R042: GVW 25,950-30,000. **W.B.** 165-217. 6 Cyl. 396 CID (6.5L) T-Diesel. Tires 10R22.5F.						
20000	Ch & Tilt Cab	7A1	$38516	9280	18000	23850
W7HV: GVW 32,900. **W.B.** 154-217. 6 Cyl. 396 CID (6.5L) T-Diesel. Tires 11R22.5G. Air Brakes						
24600	Ch & Tilt Cab (6 Spd.)	7A1	$48644	10110	22150	28775
1993 CHEVROLET-AT-PS-AC						
K1500 BLAZER: ½ Ton. 4WD GVW 6250. **W.B.** 111.5. V8 350 CID (5.7L). Tires LT225/75R16.						
16500	Utility	K18	$20005	4608	14850	19175
900	Add Sport Trim				900	900

T R U C K S

SEE PAGE T-2 FOR ADDITIONAL OPTIONS
PACIFIC NORTHWEST EDITION

c

CHEVROLET 1993 T-23

Trd-In	BODY TYPE	Model No.	M.S.R.P.	Wgt.	Loan	Retail
	1993 CHEVROLET-AT-PS-AC-Continued					
9000	Pickup Fleetside Ext. Cab 6' S19		$11630	3024	8100	11150
550	Add Tahoe Trim..				550	550
550	Deduct 4 Cyl. Engine				550	550

C1500: ½ Ton. GVW 5600-6600. **W.B.** 117.5-155.5. V8 305 CID (5.0L). Tires P225/75R15, Ext. Cab P235/75R15.

Trd-In	BODY TYPE	Model No.	M.S.R.P.	Wgt.	Loan	Retail
9700	Pickup Fleetside "WT" 8' (V6) C14		$11225		8750	11925
12100	Pickup Sportside 6½' C14		13985		10900	14500
11800	Pickup Fleetside 6½' C14		13585	3717	10625	14200
11900	Pickup Fleetside 8' C14		13885	3860	10725	14300
13600	Pickup Fleetside Ext. Cab 6½' C19		15130	4032	12250	16100
13700	Pickup Fleetside Ext. Cab 8' C19		15390	4127	12350	16200
13900	Pickup Sportside Ext. Cab 6½' C19		15530		12525	16425
15300	Pickup Fleetside "454SS" C14		21240		13775	17900

C2500: ¾ Ton. GVW 7200-8600. **W.B.** 131.5-155.5. V8 350 CID (5.7L). Tires LT225/75R16.

Trd-In	BODY TYPE	Model No.	M.S.R.P.	Wgt.	Loan	Retail
11900	Ch & Cab C24		$15569		10725	14300
12550	Pickup Fleetside 8' C24		14425	4021	11300	14975
13350	Ch & Ext. Cab C29		17244		12025	15825
14250	Pickup Fleetside Ext. Cab 6½' C29		16240	4160	12825	16775
14350	Pickup Fleetside Ext. Cab 8' C29		16520	4261	12925	16900

C3500: 1 Ton. GVW 9000-15,000. **W.B.** 131.5-183.5. V8 350 CID (5.7L), HD V8 454 CID (7.4L). Tires LT245/75R16, HD 225/70R19.5 Dual Rear Wheels.

Trd-In	BODY TYPE	Model No.	M.S.R.P.	Wgt.	Loan	Retail
12550	Ch & Cab C34		$15704		11300	15775
13200	Pickup Fleetside 8' C34		16164	4638	11900	16475
14350	Ch & Ext. Cab C39		17374		12925	17725
15000	Pickup Fleetside Ext. Cab 8' C39		17824	4874	13500	18425
15525	Pickup Fleetside Crew Cab 8' C33		18144	5176	13975	18975
14875	Ch & Crew Cab C33		17694		13400	18275
15250	Ch & Cab Heavy Duty C34		18989		13725	18700
700	Add Sport Trim				700	700
650	Add Silverado Trim				650	650
650	Add V8 6.2L Diesel Engine				650	650
950	Add V8 6.5L Turbo Diesel Engine (Std. HD)				950	950
600	Deduct V6 Engine				600	600

MEDIUM DUTY TRUCKS-5 Spd.-PS
KODIAK SERIES
C6H042 (C60): GVW 16,850-27,100. **W.B.** 132-261. (6.6L) Diesel. Tires 235/80R22.5G, LoPro 225/70R19.5F.

Trd-In	BODY TYPE	Model No.	M.S.R.P.	Wgt.	Loan	Retail
17350	Ch & Cab 6H1		$27405	6800	15625	21000
17750	Ch & Cab LoPro 6H1		26255	6523	15975	21450

C7H042 (C70): GVW 21,200-39,000. **W.B.** 144-261. (6.6L) Diesel. Tires 235/80R22.5G.

Trd-In	BODY TYPE	Model No.	M.S.R.P.	Wgt.	Loan	Retail
18200	Ch & Cab 7H1		$28345	7076	16400	21925
2700	Deduct Gas Engine				2700	2700

MEDIUM DUTY CABOVER-5 Spd.-PS
W4S042: GVW 11,050-14,250. **W.B.** 109-150. 4 Cyl. 236 CID (3.9L) T-Diesel. Tires 215/85R16E.

Trd-In	BODY TYPE	Model No.	M.S.R.P.	Wgt.	Loan	Retail
10950	Ch & Tilt Cab.................................. 4B1		$20876		9875	13950

W5R042: GVW 18,000. **W.B.** 113-177. 6 Cyl. 396 CID (6.5L) T-Diesel. Tires 215/75R17.5F.

Trd-In	BODY TYPE	Model No.	M.S.R.P.	Wgt.	Loan	Retail
12850	Ch & Tilt Cab.................................. 5B1		$27196		11575	16100

W6R042: GVW 22,000. **W.B.** 144-213. 6 Cyl. 396 CID (6.5L) T-Diesel. Tires 9R22.5F.

Trd-In	BODY TYPE	Model No.	M.S.R.P.	Wgt.	Loan	Retail
14950	Ch & Tilt Cab.................................. 6A1		$32880		13475	18375

W7R042: GVW 25,950-30,000. **W.B.** 142-217. 6 Cyl. 396 CID (6.5L) T-Diesel. Tires 10R22.5F.

Trd-In	BODY TYPE	Model No.	M.S.R.P.	Wgt.	Loan	Retail
17050	Ch & Tilt Cab.................................. 7A1		$34804		15350	20700

W7HV: GVW 32,900. **W.B.** 142-217. 6 Cyl. 396 CID (6.5L) T-Diesel. Tires 11R22.5G. **Air Brakes**

Trd-In	BODY TYPE	Model No.	M.S.R.P.	Wgt.	Loan	Retail
21450	Ch & Tilt Cab (6 Spd.) 7A1		$43244		19325	25400

SEE PAGE T-2 FOR ADDITIONAL OPTIONS
PACIFIC NORTHWEST EDITION

c

T R U C K S

Source: N.A.D.A. Official Used Car Guide®, April 1996, Pacific Northwest Edition. Used with permission of the N.A.D.A. Official Used Car Guide® Company.

T-34 **DODGE 1995-94**

Trd-In	BODY TYPE	Model No.	M.S.R.P.	Wgt.	Loan	Retail

1994 DODGE-AT-PS-AC
CARAVAN: FWD GVW 4340-5420. **W.B.** 112-119. V6 202 CID (3.3L). Tires P195/75R15, LE & Grand P205/70R14.

Trd-In	BODY TYPE	Model No.	M.S.R.P.	Wgt.	Loan	Retail
9775	Caravan C/V	H11	$14412	3135	8800	12000
10850	Extended Caravan C/V	H14	16866	3436	9775	13150
11175	Caravan	H25	14919	3308	10075	13525
12325	Caravan SE	H45	18139	3464	11100	14725
13525	Caravan LE	H55	21963	3618	12175	16025
12550	Grand Caravan	H24	18178	3574	11300	14975
13400	Grand Caravan SE	H44	19304	3581	12075	15875
14600	Grand Caravan LE	H54	22883	3788	13150	17150
1400	Add All Wheel Drive				1400	1400
225	Add 4 Wheel ABS				225	225
450	Add ES Trim				450	450
600	Deduct 4 Cyl. Engine				600	600

B150: ½ Ton. GVW 5000-6010. **W.B.** 109.6-127.6. V8 318 CID (5.2L). Tires P205/75R15.

Trd-In	BODY TYPE	Model No.	M.S.R.P.	Wgt.	Loan	Retail
13925	Wagon 109.6"	B15	$14491	4085	12550	16450
12575	Van 109.6"	B11	12951	3785	11325	15000

B250: ¾ Ton. GVW 6010-6400. **W.B.** 109.6-127.6. V8 318 CID (5.2L). Tires P225/75R15, Maxi P235/75R15.

Trd-In	BODY TYPE	Model No.	M.S.R.P.	Wgt.	Loan	Retail
14400	Wagon 127.6"	B25	$18260	4182	12975	16950
15150	Maxiwagon 127.6"	B24	19546	4571	13650	17750
12875	Van 109.6"	B21	15911	3734	11600	15325
13800	Maxivan 127.6"	B24	17266	4064	12425	16300

B350: 1 Ton. GVW 7500-9000. **W.B.** 127.6. V8 318 CID (5.2L). Tires LT225/75R16, Maxi LT225/75R16.

Trd-In	BODY TYPE	Model No.	M.S.R.P.	Wgt.	Loan	Retail
14750	Wagon 127.6"	B35	$19548	4556	13275	18150
15500	Maxiwagon 127.6"	B34	20565	4751	13950	18950

SEE PAGE T-2 FOR ADDITIONAL OPTIONS
1996 APRIL 1996

c

T R U C K S

Source: N.A.D.A. Official Used Car Guide®, April 1996, Pacific Northwest Edition. Used with permission of the N.A.D.A. Official Used Car Guide® Company.

DODGE 1994-93 T-35

Trd-In	BODY TYPE	Model No.	M.S.R.P.	Wgt.	Loan	Retail
1994 DODGE-AT-PS-AC-Continued						
13400	Van 127.6"....................B31		$17559	4218	12075	16700
14150	Maxivan 127.6"................B34		18524	4368	12750	17500
800	Add LE Trim				800	800
225	Add 4 Wheel ABS				225	225
650	Deduct V6 Engine				650	650

DAKOTA: ½ Ton. GVW 4290-6100. **W.B.** 111.9-130.9. V6 239 CID (3.9L). Tires P195/75R15, Sport & Club Cab P215/75R15.

Trd-In	BODY TYPE	Model No.	M.S.R.P.	Wgt.	Loan	Retail
9350	Pickup Sweptline "S" 6½'........L26		$9560	2991	8425	11550
9450	Pickup Sweptline "S" 8'.........L26		11085	3348	8525	11650
9950	Pickup Sweptline 6½'...........L26		11432	2991	8975	12200
10050	Pickup Sweptline 8'............L26		12282	3080	9050	12300
9650	Pickup Sweptline Sport 6½'......L26		10742	2991	8700	11875
11700	Pickup Club Cab 6½'............L23		14299	3508	10550	14075
11400	Pickup Club Cab Sport 6½'.......L23		14042	3508	10275	13750
500	Add SLT Trim				500	500
225	Add 4 Wheel ABS				225	225
650	Add V8 Engine				650	650
600	Deduct 4 Cyl. Engine				600	600

RAM 1500: ½ Ton. GVW 6100-6400. **W.B.** 119-135. V8 318 CID (5.2L). Tires P225/75R16.

Trd-In	BODY TYPE	Model No.	M.S.R.P.	Wgt.	Loan	Retail
10875	Pickup Sweptline "S" 6½' (V6)......C16		$11824	3958	9800	13175
10975	Pickup Sweptline "S" 8' (V6)........C16		12096	4121	9900	13300
13525	Pickup Sweptline 6½'............C16		14389	4035	12175	16025
13625	Pickup Sweptline 8'............C16		14661	4198	12275	16125

RAM 2500: ¾ Ton. GVW 7500-8800. **W.B.** 135. V8 360 CID (5.9L). Tires LT225/75R16.

Trd-In	BODY TYPE	Model No.	M.S.R.P.	Wgt.	Loan	Retail
13825	Heavy Duty Ch & Cab............C26		$16641	4438	12450	16325
14375	Pickup Sweptline 8'............C26		15916	4656	12950	16925
14700	Pickup Heavy Duty 8'...........C26		17102	4696	13250	17275

RAM 3500: 1 Ton. GVW 10,500-11,000. **W.B.** 135. V8 360 CID (5.9L). Tires LT215/85R16. Dual Rear Wheels.

Trd-In	BODY TYPE	Model No.	M.S.R.P.	Wgt.	Loan	Retail
15475	Ch & Cab.....................C36		$17514	5111	13950	18925
16025	Pickup Sweptline 8'............C36		18417	5212	14425	19525
200	Add ST Trim				200	200
750	Add Laramie SLT Trim				750	750
225	Add 4 Wheel ABS				225	225
2000	Add 6 Cyl. 5.9L Turbo Diesel Engine				2000	2000
450	Add V10 8.0L Engine				450	450
650	Deduct V6 Engine				650	650

1993 DODGE-AT-PS-AC

RAM 50: ½ Ton. GVW 4165-4800. **W.B.** 105-116. 4 Cyl. 144 CID (2.4L). Tires P195/75R14.

Trd-In	BODY TYPE	Model No.	M.S.R.P.	Wgt.	Loan	Retail
7025	Pickup.......................S21		$8865	2690	6325	9000
7125	Pickup LB....................S22		9432	2795	6425	9125
7425	Pickup SE....................S41		10035		6700	9450

RAMCHARGER: ½ Ton. GVW 5600-6000. **W.B.** 106. V8 318 CID (5.2L). Tires P235/75R15.

Trd-In	BODY TYPE	Model No.	M.S.R.P.	Wgt.	Loan	Retail
12225	Utility 150 S.................E07		$17636	4223	11025	14625
13900	Utility 150 S 4WD.............M07		19985	4570	12525	16425
13175	Utility 150...................E17		19926	4223	11875	15650
14850	Utility 150 4WD...............M17		21696	4580	13375	17425
700	Add LE Trim				700	700
800	Add Canyon Sport Trim				800	800

CARAVAN: FWD GVW 4220-5290. **W.B.** 112-119. V6 202 CID (3.3L). Tires P195/70R14.

Trd-In	BODY TYPE	Model No.	M.S.R.P.	Wgt.	Loan	Retail
8725	Caravan C/V...................H11		$13566	3059	7875	10850
9750	Extended Caravan C/V..........H14		16020	3293	8775	11975
10075	Caravan......................H25		14073	3275	9075	12325
11125	Caravan SE...................H45		16101		10025	13475

SEE PAGE T-2 FOR ADDITIONAL OPTIONS
PACIFIC NORTHWEST EDITION

T
R
U
C
K
S

Source: N.A.D.A. Official Used Car Guide®, April 1996, Pacific Northwest Edition. Used with permission of the N.A.D.A. Official Used Car Guide® Company.

T-36 DODGE 1993-92

Trd-In	BODY TYPE	Model No.	M.S.R.P.	Wgt.	Loan	Retail
1993 DODGE-AT-PS-AC-Continued						
12225	Caravan LE............................H55		$20841		11025	14625
11325	Grand Caravan H44		17555	3602	10200	13675
12150	Grand Caravan SE................H44		17935		10950	14550
13250	Grand Caravan LE................H54		21784		11925	15725
1300	Add All Wheel Drive.................................				1300	1300
200	Add 4 Wheel ABS.....................................				200	200
400	Add ES Trim..				400	400
550	Deduct 4 Cyl. Engine				550	550
B150: ½ Ton. GVW 5000-6010. W.B. 109-127. V8 318 CID (5.2L). Tires P205/75R15.						
12625	Wagon 109.6".......................B15		$16160	4189	11375	15050
11325	Van 109.6".............................B11		14564	3898	10200	13675
B250: ¾ Ton. GVW 6010-6400. W.B. 109-127. V8 318 CID (5.2L). Tires P225/75R15.						
13025	Wagon 127.6".......................B25		$17662	4331	11725	15475
13725	Maxiwagon 127.6"................B24		18948	4567	12375	16225
11575	Van 109.6".............................B21		15112	3875	10425	13950
12425	Maxivan 127.6".....................B24		16793	4211	11200	14850
B350: 1 Ton. GVW 7500-9000. W.B. 127. V8 318 CID (5.2L). Tires LT225/75R15.						
13375	Wagon 127.6".......................B35		$18950	4555	12050	16675
14075	Maxiwagon 127.6"................B34		19967	4749	12675	17425
12075	Van 127.6".............................B31		17086	4215	10875	15275
12775	Maxivan 127.6".....................B34		18051	4364	11500	16025
700	Add LE Trim..				700	700
600	Deduct V6 Engine....................................				600	600
DAKOTA: ½ Ton. GVW 4300-6250. W.B. 112-131. V6 239 CID (3.9L). Tires P195/75R15.						
7725	Sweptline S 6½' (4 Cyl.,5 Spd.) L16		$9154	2948	6975	9775
8950	Pickup Sweptline 6½' L26		11162	3220	8075	11100
9050	Pickup Sweptline 8'...............L26		11345	3309	8150	11225
8725	Pickup Sweptline Sport 6½'....L26		9943		7875	10850
10550	Pickup Club Cab 6½'.............L23		12414	3479	9500	12825
600	Add LE Trim..				600	600
600	Add V8 Engine...				600	600
550	Deduct 4 Cyl. Engine				550	550
D150: ½ Ton. GVW 5500-6400. W.B. 115-149. V8 318 CID (5.2L). Tires P215/75R15.						
9450	Pickup Sweptline 6½' E16		$13733	3834	8525	11650
9550	Pickup Sweptline 8'...............E16		13950	3947	8600	11750
11250	Pickup Club Cab 6½'.............E13		15815	4220	10125	13600
11350	Pickup Club Cab 8'................E13		16034	4339	10225	13700
D250: ¾ Ton. GVW 7400-8510. W.B. 131-149. V8 318 CID (5.2L). Tires LT215/85R16.						
9550	Ch & Cab...............................E26		$15122	4002	8600	11750
10200	Pickup Sweptline 8'...............E26		15010	4220	9200	12450
12000	Pickup Club Cab 8'................E23		17175	4456	10800	14400
D350: 1 Ton. GVW 8700-10,100. W.B. 131-159. V8 360 CID (5.9L). Tires LT235/85R16.						
10200	Ch & Cab...............................E36		$15602	4038	9200	13150
10850	Pickup Sweptline 8'...............E36		15876	4365	9775	13850
14250	Pickup Club Cab 8' (Diesel) E33		22060	5537	12825	17625
700	Add LE Trim..				700	700
1600	Add 6 Cyl. 5.9L Turbo Diesel Engine				1600	1600
600	Deduct V6 Engine....................................				600	600
1992 DODGE-AT-PS-AC						
RAM 50: ½ Ton. GVW 4165-4890. W.B. 105-116. 4 Cyl. 146 CID (2.4L). Tires P195/75R14.						
5825	Pickup..................................L24		$8178	2580	5250	7650
5925	Pickup LB..............................L29		8723	2690	5350	7775
6175	Pickup SE..............................L44		9298	2585	5575	8050

T
R
U
C
K
S

SEE PAGE T-2 FOR ADDITIONAL OPTIONS
1996 APRIL 1996

c

Source: N.A.D.A. Official Used Car Guide®, April 1996, Pacific Northwest Edition.
Used with permission of the N.A.D.A. Official Used Car Guide® Company.

DODGE 1992 T-37

Trd-In	BODY TYPE	Model No.	M.S.R.P.	Wgt.	Loan	Retail
1992 DODGE-AT-PS-AC-Continued						
RAMCHARGER: ½ Ton. GVW 5600-6400. W.B. 106. V8 318 CID (5.2L). Tires P235/75R15.						
9575	Utility 150 S	E07	$16545		8625	11775
11175	Utility 150 S 4WD	M07	17939		10075	13525
10475	Utility 150	E17	18764		9450	12750
12075	Utility 150 4WD	M17	19595		10875	14475
650	Add LE Trim				650	650
750	Add Canyon Sport Trim				750	750
CARAVAN: FWD GVW 4280-5340. W.B. 112-119. V6 202 CID (3.3L). Tires P195/75R14.						
7400	Caravan C/V	H11	$12820		6675	9425
8375	Extended Caravan C/V	H14	15209		7550	10475
8500	Caravan	H25	13706		7650	10625
9500	Caravan SE	H45	15679		8550	11700
10450	Caravan LE	H55	20102		9425	12725
9650	Grand Caravan	H44	17281		8700	11875
10475	Grand Caravan SE	H44	17511		9450	12750
11425	Grand Caravan LE	H54	20822		10300	13800
1200	Add All Wheel Drive				1200	1200
150	Add 4 Wheel ABS				150	150
300	Add ES Trim				300	300
500	Deduct 4 Cyl. Engine				500	500
B150: ½ Ton. GVW 5300-6010. W.B. 109-127. V8 318 CID (5.2L). Tires P205/75R15.						
10825	Wagon 109.6"	B15	$15167		9750	13125
9575	Van 109.6"	B11	13779		8625	11775
B250: ¾ Ton. GVW 6010-6400. W.B. 109-127. V8 318 CID (5.2L). Tires P225/75R15.						
11150	Wagon 127.6"	B25	$16669		10050	13500
11800	Maxiwagon 127.6"	B24	17955		10625	14200
9775	Van 109.6"	B21	14077		8800	12000
10550	Maxivan 127.6"	B24	16008		9500	12825
B350: 1 Ton. GVW 7500-9000. W.B. 127. V8 318 CID (5.2L). Tires LT225/75R16.						
11450	Wagon 127.6"	B35	$17957		10325	14550
12100	Maxiwagon 127.6"	B34	19244		10900	15300
10200	Van 127.6"	B31	15951		9200	13150
10850	Maxivan 127.6"	B34	17266		9775	13850
650	Add LE Trim				650	650
550	Deduct V6 Engine				550	550
DAKOTA: ½ Ton. GVW 4250-6210. W.B. 112-131. V6 239 CID (3.9L). Tires P195/75R15.						
6950	Sweptline S 6½' (4 Cyl., 5 Spd.)	L16	$8995		6275	8900
8050	Pickup Sweptline 6½'	L26	10705		7250	10125
8150	Pickup Sweptline 8'	L26	10988		7350	10250
9350	Pickup Club Cab 6½'	L23	11872		8425	11550
550	Add LE Trim				550	550
550	Add V8 Engine				550	550
500	Deduct 4 Cyl. Engine				500	500
D150: ½ Ton. GVW 5200-6400. W.B. 115-149. V8 318 CID (5.2L). Tires P215/75R15.						
8425	Pickup Sweptline 6½'	E16	$13083		7600	10525
8525	Pickup Sweptline 8'	E16	13300		7675	10650
9975	Pickup Club Cab 6½'	E13	15165		9000	12225
10075	Pickup Club Cab 8'	E13	15384		9075	12325
D250: ¾ Ton. GVW 7400-8510. W.B. 131-149. V8 318 CID (5.2L). Tires LT215/85R16.						
8375	Ch & Cab	E26	$14343		7550	10475
9075	Pickup Sweptline 8'	E26	14241		8175	11250
10625	Pickup Club Cab 8'	E23	16925		9575	12900
D350: 1 Ton. GVW 8700-11,000. W.B. 131-159. V8 360 CID (5.9L). Tires LT235/85R16.						
9025	Ch & Cab	E36	$14833		8125	11800
9725	Pickup Sweptline 8'	E36	15790		8775	12575

T R U C K S

SEE PAGE T-2 FOR ADDITIONAL OPTIONS
PACIFIC NORTHWEST EDITION

c

Source: N.A.D.A. Official Used Car Guide®, April 1996, Pacific Northwest Edition. Used with permission of the N.A.D.A. Official Used Car Guide® Company.

FORD 1995-94 T-43

Trd-In	BODY TYPE	Model No.	M.S.R.P.	Wgt.	Loan	Retail

1994 FORD-AT-PS-AC
EXPLORER: ½ Ton. GVW 4780-5420. W.B. 102-112. V6 245 CID (4.0L). Tires P225/70R15SL.

Trd-In	BODY TYPE	Model No.	M.S.R.P.	Wgt.	Loan	Retail
14000	Wagon 2D	U22	$17240	3646	12600	16525
15200	Wagon 4D	U32	18130	3844	13700	17800
15700	Wagon 2D 4WD	U24	18990	3863	14150	18325
16900	Wagon 4D 4WD	U34	19900	4053	15225	19600
600	Add Sport Trim				600	600
900	Add XLT Trim				900	900

SEE PAGE T-2 FOR ADDITIONAL OPTIONS
PACIFIC NORTHWEST EDITION

T R U C K S

Source: N.A.D.A. Official Used Car Guide®, April 1996, Pacific Northwest Edition. Used with permission of the N.A.D.A. Official Used Car Guide® Company.

FORD 1994-93 T-45

Trd-In	BODY TYPE	Model No.	M.S.R.P.	Wgt.	Loan	Retail
1994 FORD-AT-PS-AC-Continued						
13825	Pickup Styleside Lightning 6¾'	F15	$21627		**12450**	**16325**
11750	Pickup Styleside 8'	F15	14180	3980	**10575**	**14125**
11700	Pickup Styleside Supercab "S" 6¾'	X15	14119		**10550**	**14075**
11800	Pickup Styleside Supercab "S" 8'	X15	14353		**10625**	**14200**
14100	Pickup Flareside Supercab 6¾'	X15	16268	4268	**12700**	**16625**
13700	Pickup Styleside Supercab 6¾'	X15	15562	4196	**12350**	**16200**
13800	Pickup Styleside Supercab 8'	X15	15805	4321	**12425**	**16300**
F250: ¾ Ton. GVW 6600-8800. **W.B.** 133-155. V8 351 CID (5.8L). Tires LT215/85R16D, HD LT235/85R16E.						
12500	Pickup Styleside 8'	F25	$14802	4252	**11250**	**14925**
12800	Pickup Heavy Duty 8'	F25	15369	4481	**11525**	**15250**
13550	Pickup Heavy Duty Supercab "S" 8'	X25	16456		**12200**	**16050**
14550	Pickup Heavy Duty Supercab 8'	X25	17900	4761	**13100**	**17100**
F350: 1 Ton. GVW 9000-11,000. **W.B.** 133-168.4. V8 351 CID (5.8L). Supercab V8 460 CID (7.5L). Tires LT235/85R16D, F35, X35 Dual Rear Wheels LT215/85R16D.						
12650	Ch & Cab	F37	$15437	4116	**11400**	**15900**
14025	Pickup Styleside 8'	F35	17639	4872	**12625**	**17375**
15825	Pickup Styleside Crew Cab 8'	W35	19341	5212	**14250**	**19300**
16925	Pickup Styleside Supercab 8'	X35	19732	5399	**15250**	**20500**
SUPER DUTY: 1 Ton. GVW 15,000-17,000. **W.B.** 136.8-228. V8 460 CID (7.5L). Tires LT235/85R16E. Dual Rear Wheels.						
15750	Ch & Cab (5 Spd.)	F47	$20398	5521	**14175**	**19225**
850	Add XLT Trim				**850**	**850**
1100	Add V8 7.3L Diesel Engine				**1100**	**1100**
1950	Add V8 7.3L Turbo Diesel Engine (Std. X35, F47)				**1950**	**1950**
650	Deduct 6 Cyl. Engine				**650**	**650**
MEDIUM DUTY TRUCKS-5 Spd.-PS						
F600: GVW 21,000-28,000. **W.B.** 129-255. 6 Cyl. 359 CID (5.9L). Dsl. Tires 11R22.5.						
20000	Ch & Cab	F60	$24704	6296	**18000**	**23850**
F700: GVW 22,200-35,000. **W.B.** 129-256. 6 Cyl. 359 CID (5.9L). Dsl. Tires 9R22.5.						
20900	Ch & Cab	F70	$25629	6649	**18825**	**24800**
LN7000: GVW 24,500-35,000. **W.B.** 138-258. 6 Cyl. 359 CID (5.9L). Dsl. Tires 10R22.5. **Air Brakes**						
21700	Ch & Cab	R72	$41379	8000	**19550**	**25675**
CF7000: GVW 24,800-33,000. **W.B.** 153-225. 6 Cyl. 359 CID (5.9L). Dsl. Tires 9R22.5. **Air Brakes**						
22700	Ch & Cab	H70	$41235	9327	**20450**	**26750**
3000	Deduct Gas Engine (F600/F700)				**3000**	**3000**
1993 FORD-AT-PS-AC						
EXPLORER: ½ Ton. GVW 4780-5380. **W.B.** 102-112. V6 245 CID (4.0L). Tires P225/70R15SL.						
12100	Wagon 2D	U22	$16652	3679	**10900**	**14500**
13200	Wagon 4D	U32	17416	3858	**11900**	**15675**
13775	Wagon 2D 4WD	U24	18458	3890	**12400**	**16275**
14875	Wagon 4D 4WD	U34	19246	3997	**13400**	**17450**
550	Add Sport Trim				**550**	**550**
800	Add XLT Trim				**800**	**800**
1450	Add Eddie Bauer Trim				**1450**	**1450**
2100	Add Limited Trim				**2100**	**2100**
BRONCO: ½ Ton. 4WD GVW 6050. **W.B.** 104.7. V8 302 CID (5.0L). Tires P235/75R15XL.						
15350	Wagon	U15	$20084	4574	**13825**	**17950**
800	Add XLT Trim				**800**	**800**
1450	Add Eddie Bauer Trim				**1450**	**1450**
AEROSTAR: ½ Ton. GVW 4920-5340. **W.B.** 119. V6 182 CID (3.0L). Tires P215/70R14SL.						
8225	Cargo Van	A14	$14221	3296	**7425**	**10325**
9825	Wagon	A11	14416	3481	**8850**	**12050**
8325	Window Van	A15	14516		**7500**	**10425**
9400	Extended Cargo Van	A34	14968	3390	**8475**	**11600**

SEE PAGE T-2 FOR ADDITIONAL OPTIONS
PACIFIC NORTHWEST EDITION

c

TRUCKS

Source: N.A.D.A. Official Used Car Guide®, April 1996, Pacific Northwest Edition. Used with permission of the N.A.D.A. Official Used Car Guide® Company.

T-46 FORD 1993

Trd-In	BODY TYPE	Model No.	M.S.R.P.	Wgt.	Loan	Retail
1993 FORD-AT-PS-AC-Continued						
11000	Extended Wagon A31		$16208	3558	9900	13325
9500	Extended Window Van A35		15264		8550	11700
800	Add XLT Trim				800	800
1450	Add Eddie Bauer Trim				1450	1450
1300	Add All Wheel Drive				1300	1300

CLUB WAGON E150/E350: ½-1 Ton. GVW 6700-9300. W.B. 138. V8 351 CID (5.8L). Tires P235/75R15XL, E350 LT245/75R16E.

Trd-In	BODY TYPE	Model No.	M.S.R.P.	Wgt.	Loan	Retail
13250	Club Wagon E150 .... E11		$17459	5022	11925	15725
13850	Club Wagon E350 .... E31		18446	5484	12475	16350
14550	Super Club Wagon E350 .... S31		20497	5697	13100	17100
800	Add XLT Trim				800	800
1450	Add Chateau Trim				1450	1450
1000	Add V8 7.3L Diesel Engine				1000	1000
600	Deduct 6 Cyl. Engine				600	600

ECONOLINE E150: ½ Ton. GVW 5500-6700. W.B. 138. V8 302 CID (5.0L). Tires P215/75R15SL.

Trd-In	BODY TYPE	Model No.	M.S.R.P.	Wgt.	Loan	Retail
10875	Cargo Van 138" E14		$15436	4450	9800	13175

ECONOLINE E250: ¾ Ton. GVW 7200-8550. W.B. 138. V8 351 CID (5.8L). Tires LT225/75R16D.

Trd-In	BODY TYPE	Model No.	M.S.R.P.	Wgt.	Loan	Retail
11125	Cargo Van 138" E24		$16093	4966	10025	13475
11825	Super Cargo Van 138" S24		16743	5109	10650	14225

ECONOLINE E350: 1 Ton. GVW 9300-11,500. W.B. 138-176. V8 351 CID (5.8L). Tires LT245/75R16E.

Trd-In	BODY TYPE	Model No.	M.S.R.P.	Wgt.	Loan	Retail
11475	Cargo Van 138" E34		$17192	5177	10350	14575
12175	Super Cargo Van 138" S34		18103	5285	10975	15375
11700	Cutaway 138" E37		17010	5184	10550	14800
400	Add XL Trim				400	400
1000	Add V8 7.3L Diesel Engine				1000	1000
600	Deduct 6 Cyl. Engine				600	600

RANGER: ½ Ton. GVW 4220-5040. W.B. 108-125. V6 182 CID (3.0L). Tires P195/70R14SL.

Trd-In	BODY TYPE	Model No.	M.S.R.P.	Wgt.	Loan	Retail
8050	Pickup Styleside R10		$8781	2918	7250	10125
8150	Pickup Styleside LB R10		9026	2955	7350	10250
9250	Pickup Flareside Splash R10		12175	3260	8325	11425
9650	Pickup Styleside Supercab R14		11775	3208	8700	11875
450	Add XLT Trim				450	450
650	Add STX Trim				650	650
550	Deduct 4 Cyl. Engine				550	550

F150: ½ Ton. GVW 5000-6250. W.B. 117-155. V8 302 CID (5.0L). Tires P215/75R15SL, Supercab P235/75R15XL.

Trd-In	BODY TYPE	Model No.	M.S.R.P.	Wgt.	Loan	Retail
8400	Styleside S 6¾' (6 Cyl.) F15		$11033		7575	10500
8500	Styleside S 8' (6 Cyl.) F15		11268		7650	10625
10800	Pickup Flareside 6¾' F15		13916	3995	9725	13100
10500	Pickup Styleside 6¾' F15		13066	3848	9450	12775
12550	Pickup Styleside Lightning 6¾' F15		21655		11300	14975
10600	Pickup Styleside 8' F15		13310	3960	9550	12875
12600	Pickup Flareside Supercab 6¾' X15		15215	4344	11350	15025
12300	Pickup Styleside Supercab 6¾' X15		14505	4164	11075	14700
12400	Pickup Styleside Supercab 8' X15		14739	4280	11175	14825

F250: ¾ Ton. GVW 6600-8800. W.B. 133-155. V8 351 CID (5.8L). Tires LT215/85R16D, HD LT235/85R16E.

Trd-In	BODY TYPE	Model No.	M.S.R.P.	Wgt.	Loan	Retail
11250	Pickup Styleside 8' F25		$14174	4219	10125	13600
11500	Pickup Heavy Duty 8' F25		14925	4448	10350	13875
13050	Pickup Heavy Duty Supercab 8' X25		17381	4718	11750	15500

SEE PAGE T-2 FOR ADDITIONAL OPTIONS
1996 APRIL 1996

c

TRUCKS

*Source: N.A.D.A. Official Used Car Guide®, April 1996, Pacific Northwest Edition.
Used with permission of the N.A.D.A. Official Used Car Guide® Company.*

FORD 1993-92 T-47

Trd-In	BODY TYPE	Model No.	M.S.R.P.	Wgt.	Loan	Retail
1993 FORD-AT-PS-AC-Continued						
F350: 1 Ton. GVW 8800-11,000. W.B. 133-168. V8 351 CID (5.8L), Supercab (7.5L). Tires LT235/85R16E, F35, X35 Dual Rear Wheels LT215/85R16D.						
11250	Ch & Cab..F37		$14997	4114	**10125**	**14325**
12600	Pickup Styleside 8'.........................F35		17046	4892	**11350**	**15850**
14225	Pickup Styleside Crew Cab 8'..........W35		18406	5178	**12825**	**17600**
15200	Pickup Styleside Supercab 8'.......... X35		18973	5329	**13700**	**18625**
SUPER DUTY: 1 Ton. GVW 15,000-17,000. W.B. 137-228. V8 460 CID (7.5L). Tires LT235/85R16E. Dual Rear Wheels.						
13900	Ch & Cab (5 Spd.) F47		$19645	5533	**12525**	**17250**
800	Add XLT Trim				**800**	**800**
1000	Add V8 7.3L Diesel Engine (Std. X35, F47)				**1000**	**1000**
600	Deduct 6 Cyl. Engine				**600**	**600**
MEDIUM DUTY TRUCKS-5 Spd.-PS						
F600: GVW 21,000-28,000. W.B. 129-256. 6 Cyl. 401 CID (6.6L) Dsl. Tires 9R22.5.						
17950	Ch & Cab..F60		$29692		**16175**	**21650**
F700: GVW 22,200-35,000. W.B. 129-256. 6 Cyl. 401 CID (6.6L) Dsl. Tires 9R22.5.						
18750	Ch & Cab..F70		$33067	7023	**16875**	**22500**
LN7000: GVW 24,500-35,000. W.B. 138-225. 6 Cyl. 401 CID (6.6L) Dsl. Tires 10R22.5 Air Brakes						
19000	Ch & Cab..R72		$36615		**17100**	**22775**
CF7000: GVW 24,800-33,000. W.B. 153-225. 6 Cyl. 401 CID (6.6L) Dsl. Tires 9R22.5. Air Brakes						
19900	Ch & Cab..H70		$36216		**17925**	**23750**
2700	Deduct Gas Engine (F600/F700)				**2700**	**2700**

Source: N.A.D.A. Official Used Car Guide®, April 1996, Pacific Northwest Edition. Used with permission of the N.A.D.A. Official Used Car Guide® Company.

Notes:

Most people place the process of purchasing a car right up there with changing the litter box. And as the Saturn philosophy of automobile buying—the non-negotiations, no hassles method—continue to become more popular, consumers are anxious to master the art of getting to the heart of the matter.

Enter this instructional video, which was created by a veteran automobile salesman who talks his way through the nitty-gritty details: buying new vs. used, trade-ins, warranties, dealership profit, and more. Charts and other explanatory methods are liberally used, production values are laudable for a home-grown video, and the information is useful and succinctly presented.

Cathrine Applefeld, *Billboard Magazine*

"Anyone thinking about buying a car or truck should find this video useful."

Gary L. Cheatham
Video Rating Guide for Libraries

How To Buy A Car Or Truck And Not Get Ripped Off! is the perfect companion to *Car Buying & Leasing 101.*

Use this enlightening 34-minute video to welcome Charles DeVorak into your living room, where he'll personally instruct you in buying new or used, buy backs, trading or selling your old car, negotiating the purchase price, dealer invoices, warranties, and more.

For your copy, use the enclosed order form or call the number below.

Order Form

Please photocopy this form if additional copies are needed.

Description	Price	Quantity	Total
Tapes			
How To Buy A Car Or Truck And Not Get Ripped Off	$19.95		
Books			
Car Buying & Leasing 101	$8.95		

Subtotal .... $_____

Shipping ($3.00 per item)....... $_____

Utah Residents
Add 6 1/4% Sales Tax .... $_____

TOTAL .... $_____

Payment Method:

☐ Check ☐ Money Order ☐ Visa ☐ MasterCard ☐ AMEX

Card #: _____ Exp._____

Print Cardholder's Name: _____

I authorize Vehicle Information Systems to charge the above cited credit card in the amount indicated.

Signature: _____

Payable to:
V.I.S.

6911 South 1300 East, #228 • Salt Lake City, UT 84047

Ship to:

Name _____

Address _____

City _____ St _____ Zip _____

Day Phone (_____) _____

Evening Phone (_____) _____

Prices subject to change without notice. Please allow 2-4 weeks for delivery.

Fax to 1-801-568-9494 or Call 1-800-934-3113

Order Form

Please photocopy this form if additional copies are needed.

Description	Price	Quantity	Total
Tapes			
How To Buy A Car Or Truck And Not Get Ripped Off	$19.95		
Books			
Car Buying & Leasing 101	$8.95		

Subtotal .... $_____

Shipping ($3.00 per item)....... $_____

Utah Residents
Add 6 1/4% Sales Tax .... $_____

TOTAL .... $_____

Payment Method:

☐ Check ☐ Money Order ☐ Visa ☐ MasterCard ☐ AMEX

Card #: _____ Exp._____

Print Cardholder's Name: _____

I authorize Vehicle Information Systems to charge the above cited credit card in the amount indicated.

Signature: _____

Payable to:
V.I.S.
6911 South 1300 East, #228 • Salt Lake City, UT 84047

Ship to:

Name _____

Address _____

City _____ St _____ Zip _____

Day Phone (_____) _____

Evening Phone (_____) _____

Prices subject to change without notice. Please allow 2-4 weeks for delivery.

Fax to 1-801-568-9494 or Call 1-800-934-3113

If Buying A Vehicle is STILL the Most Dreadful Experience in Your Life...

..Then you may want o consider Vehicle nformation Systems' 'urchasing Assistance 'rogram.

You've read Charles DeVorak's book, id you may have watched his video. But u're STILL reluctant to go to a dealership 1 your own or maybe you're just short of me. We can help.

Let V.I.S. negotiate the entire buying process for u. After completing a simple application, V.I.S. will t on the phone with a dealer near you and complete the ttire transaction—including the financing.

If you choose to shop on your own, we'll give you price guidance and concile the numbers associated with your transaction price, payments, etc.

All of this for a nominal fee of just $150.

If Mr. DeVorak's book and tape make buying or leasing a vehicle easy, then e Purchasing Assistance Program is one of the most convenient ways to rchase a vehicle (in fact, home delivery is available for an additional fee).

Call 1-800-934-3113 if you'd like to participate in the Purchasing sistance Program, or simply complete and return the enclosed application.

Purchasing Assistance Program Application

Please photocopy this form if additional copies are needed.

Applicant's Information:

Name _____

Address _____

City _____ St _____ Zip _____

Day Phone (_____) _____

Evening Phone (_____) _____

Vehicle Checklist:

Tell us about the vehicle you'd like to purchase/lease:

Vehicle brand _____ Year/Model _____ engine size _____

equipment package _____

color _____ ☐ 4 door ☐ 2 door Would you like 4-wheel drive? ☐ Yes ☐ No

Do you want to: ☐ purchase ☐ lease ☐ lease with a purchase option

Tell us about the vehicle you have to trade in (if any):

Vehicle brand _____ Year/Model _____ engine size _____

equipment package _____

color _____ ☐ 4 door ☐ 2 door Is it 4-wheel drive? ☐ Yes ☐ No

Mileage _____ Are service records available? ☐ Yes ☐ No

Loan Payoff (if any) $_____

Payment Method:

I grant you permission to negotiate on my behalf for the purpose of obtaining a vehicle for my purchase. I understand the guidelines suggested in the book, Car Buying & Leasing 101, will be utilized in the transaction you'll be structuring for me. I understand the fee for the Purchasing Assistance Program is $150 per vehicle.

☐ Check ☐ Money Order ☐ Visa ☐ MasterCard ☐ AMEX

Card #: _____ Exp._____

Print Cardholder's Name: _____

I authorize Vehicle Information Systems to charge the above cited credit card in the amount indicated.

Signature: _____

Payable to:

V.I.S. • 6911 South 1300 East, #228 • Salt Lake City, UT 84047

Price subject to change without notice.

Fax to 1-801-568-9494 or Call 1-800-934-3113